A Suitable Amount of Crime

Nils Christie

Routledge
Taylor & Francis Group

LONDON AND NEW YORK

First published 2004
by Routledge
11 New Fetter Lane, London EC4P 4EE

Simultaneously published in the USA and Canada
by Routledge
29 West 35th Street, New York, NY 10001

Routledge is an imprint of the Taylor & Francis Group

© 2004 Nils Christie

Typeset in Goudy by BC Typesetting Ltd, Bristol
Printed and bound in Great Britain by
TJ International Ltd, Padstow, Cornwall

British Library Cataloguing in Publication Data
A catalogue record for this book is available from the British Library

Library of Congress Cataloging in Publication Data
A catalog record for this book has been requested

ISBN 0–415–33610–4 (hbk)
ISBN 0–415–33611–2 (pbk)

Contents

A Suitable Amount of Crime

Deplorable acts exist but does crime exist? If it does, how much is too much?

Crime is not a fixed concept and which acts are considered criminal varies historically and between societies. Any act can be defined as criminal, so crime is theoretically in endless supply.

A Suitable Amount of Crime looks at the great variations between countries in what are considered 'unwanted acts', how many are constructed as criminal and how many are punished. It describes the differences between Eastern and Western Europe and between the USA and the rest of the world. The author denounces the size of prison populations in punitive states as a threat to human values and civil forms of societies and proposes that academics and researchers have a moral obligation to highlight that alternatives exist.

Nils Christie is a world-renowned criminologist whose work has been published in a great number of languages. This book brings together the author's years of experience studying crime and penal systems. It is written in an engaging and easily accessible style and will appeal to anyone interested in understanding contemporary problems of crime and punishment.

Roots

So many writers circle around the same theme for much of their lives. Central for me has been the meaning of crime. What sort of phenomenon is it? Deplorable acts exist, but does crime exist? What do we mean when we say so, and under what conditions do we say it?

This was a theme for my very first piece of research, a study of guards in concentration camps.[1] How did the guards perceive their own actions? How did those among them who later were sentenced for maltreatment and killing in the camps look at their own acts at the time when they occurred? Was it crime, as they saw it? It was not, and I tried to describe why they saw what they saw. Later followed studies of people sentenced to years of forced labour due to repeated heavy drinking in public places.[2] There was a strong wish to get rid of these drinkers, but the nuisance was not sufficient to result in imprisonment. But what could not be done against them if their acts were seen as crimes became possible when their acts were seen as symptoms of sickness and forced labour seen as a health measure. Parallel phenomena occurred in the field of drugs.[3] Here the questions became: When is a substance a drug, and what is it that makes the sale of certain drugs a crime and others for membership in the Chamber of Commerce?

And then, to the other end of this problem: Concepts have consequences. I have for several years kept track of prison developments within modern industrialized countries.[4] There exist great variations between countries, and also within countries over time. How to understand these? The size of the prison population is often seen as a reflection of the crime situation in a country. But if crime is so difficult to define, how then to explain the variation in the number of prisoners? Perhaps this problem can be turned into an explanation. Since crime does not exist as a stable entity, the crime concept is well suited to all sorts of control purposes. It is like a sponge. The term can absorb a lot of acts – and people – when external circumstances make that useful. But it can also be brought to reduce its content, whenever suitable for those with a hand on the sponge. This understanding opens up for new questions. It opens up for a discussion of when enough is enough. It paves the way for a discussion of what is a suitable amount of crime.

So much is crime, and nothing. Crime is a concept free for use. The challenge is to understand its use within various systems, and through this understanding be able to evaluate its use and its users.

*   *   *

Some of what here is written has earlier been presented in lectures or seminars, particularly in East and West of Europe, and in South and North of America. I have been met with great kindness and stimulating comments during these meetings. Lecturing is, in fortunate cases, a two-way process. I have learned much from these encounters. For obvious reasons, I cannot here thank all those who have taken part in this life-long process, but I hope that some will see that they are here, in these pages.[5] But three exceptions have to be made. Three persons mean so much to me and also for this book, that I want to express my deep gratitude. It is to my friend in Finland, Kettil Bruun, who even after his death continues as a living moral source. It is to Stan Cohen, one of my oldest friends and a source of so much inspiration. And it is to Hedda, with all she stands for.

1 Crime does not exist[1]

1.1 Acts

We are four and a half million people in Norway. In 1955, we got our first statistics on crime reported to the police.[2] The figure was shocking: close to 30,000 cases were reported. In 2002, the figure was 320,000. The number of persons linked to these crimes has increased from 8,000 to 30,000, the number of those punished has increased from 5,000 to 20,000, and the prison population has doubled compared to its lowest point after World War II.

Does this mean that crime has increased? I do not know! And more important: I will never know!

1.2 The suffocated wife

As reported from Stockholm,[3] a man drugged his wife, thereafter causing her death through suffocation. Then he wrote to the police, told them what he had done, and also what would be the end of the story. He would board the boat to Finland, load heavy stones on his body and jump. The letter reached the police two days later. They found the entrance door to the apartment unlocked, as the man had said in his letter. They also found his wife, as he had said. The body was cared for in the old-fashioned way – cleaned, and left with a linen cloth over the face. She was 86, he 78. She had Alzheimer's. He had nursed her for a long time but now she was about to be sent away. They were very close, said the family doctor. We look for the man, he is under strong suspicion for having committed a pre-planned murder, said the police.

* * *

To some this is a story of Romeo and Juliet. To others, it is one of plain murder. Let me illustrate what might be behind these contrasting interpretations by turning to some occurrences where central authority collapses.

1.3 The fall of central authority

Ralf Dahrendorf (1985, pp. 1–3) opens his Hamlyn lecture on *Law and Order* with a powerful description of the fall of Berlin in April 1945:

> Suddenly, it became clear that there was no authority left, none at all.

Shops were found deserted, and Dahrendorf remembers:

> I still have the five slim volumes of romantic poetry, which I acquired on that occasion. Acquired? Everyone carried bags and suitcases full of stolen things home. Stolen? Perhaps taken is more correct, because even the word stealing seemed to have lost its meaning.

But, of course, it did not last:

> The supreme, horrible moment of utter lawlessness was but a holding of breath between two regimes which were breathing equally heavily down the spines of their subjects. Like the fearful ecstasy of revolution, the moment passed. While yesterday's absolute law became tomorrow's absolute injustice – and yesterday's injustice tomorrow's law – there was a brief pause of anomie, a few days, no more, with a few weeks of either side first to disassemble then to re-establish norms.

My own memories of surrendering capitals are different. My memories are from Oslo, exactly five years earlier. During the night of 9 April 1940, alarms had continuously sounded to warn us that bombs might fall. I can still feel in my stomach how relieved I was: Now my father would have no time to fuss about a dangerous looking letter which remained undelivered in my pocket, a letter, I believed, about my lack of progress in the German language. And soon more good news followed: The school was closed and was to remain so. On my way home from that closed school I got an unexpected opportunity to practise my bad German. A car stopped. Two German officers asked politely for my assistance to find an address. Equally politely, I helped them.

It was not until months later that I had internalized the lesson that the occupiers were never to be answered, except in cases where they could be given false directions. It also took a long time to understand, not only intellectually, that a theft from the enemy was no theft. Or to understand, again also with my body, that one of the most respected youth leaders in the local neighbourhood was a member of Quisling's party and therefore never to be talked to, not even given a nod when you met him. I am afraid I never quite managed. Maybe it was he I saw five years later, on the day of liberation, close in time to Dahrendorf's experience in Berlin. There was a man at some distance, running for the forest. The Criminal. While we, who had not sinned, rushed to the centre of town to celebrate the heroes released from prison.

I do not feel quite at home in Dahrendorf's Berlin. His picture is one where anomie is the exception. A few unbelievable days where the old rules were non-valid. Then came new rules. Ready-made from the state, as the old ones were. From one regime to another. The picture is one of a society where humans are controlled from above with the same strength as in the types of military camps Foucault (1977) describes as the proto-type of discipline. A tightly run panopticon.

My childhood experience, and similar ones have been added up to this day, is a life where norms are shaped, re-shaped and kept alive through a long and complicated process of interaction. Norms are not, they become. I therefore feel more at home in Hans Magnus Enzenberger's (1985) description of social life in Hungary than in Dahrendorf's from Berlin. Enzenberger describes a society where obscurities reign, where moral matters are continuously up for debate and where compromises are essential conditions for survival. Crime here becomes a shallow con-cept, hopelessly imprecise compared to the subtle distinctions and under-standings needed.

Heinz Steinert (1986) takes the word 'trouble' as his point of departure. Crime is not useful as a point of departure. But people have troubles and create troubles. And we have to do something with these troubles. The danger is too hastily to define troubles as crime. By doing so, we lose sight of interesting alternatives. We might move even one step further away from the concept of crime and say as follows: Our basic point of departure ought to be *acts*. The next step, then, is to investigate what sorts of acts that are seen as bad. Then follows an analysis of these acts perceived as bad – a classificatory scheme with categories as irritations, unpleasantness, disgust, sin – and then, but only as one among so many alternatives – crime. When crime is the last concept in the line, it is easier to raise the analytical questions: What are the social conditions for acts to be designated as crimes?

Crime does not exist. Only acts exist, acts often given different mean-ings within various social frameworks. Acts, and the meaning given them, are our data. Our challenge is to follow the destiny of acts through the universe of meanings.[4] Particularly, what are the social conditions that encourage or prevent giving the acts the meaning of being crime?

Ralf Dahrendorf's days of liberation – those days where 'there was no authority left, none at all' – those days were few. To Dahrendorf, it was 'but a holding of breath between two regimes'. To Enzenberger, and the group of Hungarians he describes, at least certain elements of those days of liberation are there forever. Regimes are in existence, but in a changing existence. Norms are there, and laws, but norms and laws open for a variety of interpretations. For Dahrendorf, this is different. The norms become an end-product, something given, as when he says: 'If the notion of law is to make any sense at all, it refers to rules which apply absolutely. Either certain forms of behaviour are ruled out as contrary to the law, and are therefore sanctioned, or not' (p. 68). He has gone a long way since he acquired his five slim volumes of romantic poetry in Berlin in 1945.

*   *   *

But this is war. Some might say that in peace norms are more stable. What is seen as crime has a more robust foundation. I am not so sure. Let us turn our attention to a Scandinavia in peace:

1.4 The man in the park

The arena for what here is to be described[5] is a small park surrounded by apartment buildings. It is in June, the month for celebration of light and sun and summer up in the North. It is a Sunday before noon, 'church-hours' is the old-fashioned term for these most quiet hours of the week. On several balconies facing the park, people enjoy late breakfasts, or are reading or relaxing.

A man arrives in the park. He carries plastic bags and sits down amid them. They contain beer bottles. He opens one bottle, two and then several, talks a bit to himself, then to some kids who soon gather around him. He talks and sings, to the enjoyment of his audience.

After a while, the man stands up, moves towards some bushes and opens his fly-buttons. Several of the kids move with him.

And here we need two apartment-buildings, not one, to get our point across: The two houses facing the park are looking exactly similar, built as they are according to the same set of plans. But their histories are not the same. One house was built in the modern way, by a professional building company. All was ready when the tenants moved in, totally finished with key in the door and an efficient lift from the garage up to each floor. Let us call it *The House of Perfection*. The other building had a more turbulent history. The builder went bankrupt. There was no more money left. No lifts that functioned, no entrance doors in the hallways, no kitchens installed – altogether a desperate situation. The prospective tenants – they had paid before the bankruptcy – were forced to remedy the worst defects. Joint actions were taken to fix doors and defective ceilings and floors, and a pathway of mud; crisis committees were created to sue the builder. It was heavy work and enforced sociability. Let us call this building *The House of Turbulence*.

And now back to the man in the park.

A man, halfway hidden in the bushes, surrounded by kids, opening his buttons is a situation open for highly different interpretations. In *The House of Turbulence*, the case was clear. The man in the bush is Peter, son of Anna. He had an accident when he was little, behaves generally a bit strangely, but is as kind as the midsummer night is long. When he drinks too much, it is just to phone his family and someone comes to take him home. In *The House of Perfection*, the situation is different. Nobody knows him. A strange man surrounded by kids. He exposes his penis. Decent onlookers from the balconies rush to telephones and call the police. A case of indecent exposure was registered, a serious sex case probably prevented.

What else could they do, the good neighbours in *The House of Perfection*, handicapped as they were by modernity? Their builder had not gone bankrupt. They were not forced to co-operate with neighbours. They were not forced to borrow tools from each other, to care for the neighbours' kids while some others spread asphalt on the pathway, to meet in endless sessions on how not to lose even more in the bankruptcy. They were not forced to get to know each other, to create a system for co-operation and at the same time a stock of shared information. So, knowledge of Peter and Anna could not disperse in their house as it did in the other house. They were, as conscientious citizens, left with only one alternative: to call the police. Peter became a potential criminal due to the lack of bankruptcy in *The House of Perfection*, while in *The House of Turbulence* he would have been helped home to Mum. Or, in a general formulation: Limited amount of knowledge inside a social system opens for the possibility of giving an act the meaning of crime.

This has consequences for the perception of what is crime and who are the criminals. You will in social systems with much internal communication gain more information concerning people around you. Among people unknown to each other, official functionaries for control become the only alternatives. But such functionaries produce crime through their existence. The penal institution is in an analogous situation to King Midas. All he touched became gold, and, as we know, he died from starvation. Much of what the police touch and all that the prisons touch, become crimes and criminals, and alternative interpretations of acts and actors might fade away. In this type of society, one's own survival activities might also be slightly outside the legally accepted zone. A broad network will also increase chances that you now and then come across people defined by authorities as criminals. We are thus back to my general theme: Acts *are* not, they *become*. People *are* not, they *become*. A broad social network with links in all directions creates at least uncertainty about what is crime and also who are the criminals.

*   *   *

The neighbours in *The House of Perfection* lived a modern life. They lived in houses where they became isolated from their neighbours. That meant that they also became isolated from information on local matters. This lack of information forced them to call the police. The case became a criminal case because these neighbours knew too little.

1.5 Daughters and husbands

Most children will, now and then, act in ways that according to the law might be considered criminal. Money might, unauthorized, disappear from mother's purse. It became clear that one of the kids had taken the money. Or kids fight – with bloody noses and destruction of family property as visible results. But mostly, we do not apply categories from penal law. Mostly, we do not call the acts crimes. Mostly, we do not call the children criminals.

Why not?

It just does not feel right.

Again, why not?

Because we know too much. We know the child from myriads of other situations. We know her usual generosity, we know her care of siblings, her joys and sorrows. A label from criminal law just would not stick; there is no space left on her forehead where such a stigma might be branded.

What happened here might be kept within the framework of the family. But sometimes the occurrences might also become known outside the family. Modern life can be seen as arenas where a whole army of providers of meaning are in attendance. Various specialists might enter. They can be seen as providers of services. But they can also be seen as in competition for giving the phenomena the type of meaning seen as relevant or natural within their particular profession. In the health system – let us think of an extreme case of panicked parents and insensitive professionals – some of the acts might be seen as indicators of an emerging deviant personality – some sort of psychiatric counselling might follow.

Within the legal system, let us think that worst came to worst, some acts by youngsters might be seen as theft or violence where police, court, and possible punishment might follow. Crime does not exist until the act has passed through some highly specialized meaning creating processes and, in the core case, ended up as occurrences certified by penal law judges as the particular type of unwanted acts called crime. Crime is one, but only one, among the numerous ways of classifying deplorable acts.

The daughter in the house is to most of us a relatively easy case illustrating the beneficial effect of closeness in such situations. Here is no space for crime. Our children are above it, except in the most extreme cases. But what is easy here creates trouble for many a woman when the man is violent. He is big, he has power, and he is dangerous. He will often isolate the woman to keep his definition of the situation the valid one; he is in his own view not violent, he is only disciplining her. She might be dependent on his continued support, or even remember days of love and therefore succumb to his definition. Intimacy might protect against perceiving the acts as crimes. This is not necessarily an advantage, seen from the woman's point of view. This book has as part of its theme the analysis of what is suitable to see as crime. Our point is that this is an open question, open for discussion, and particularly something to be seen against our values. But our reasoning is not a denial that the crime concept in certain situations and for certain purposes might prove the right one to apply. This is particularly so when there exists inequality of power between the parties. I return to this in Chapter 6.

1.6 The old school, and the new

In my days of school, an episode occurred again and again. Place: The schoolyard. Time: The major break in the middle of the day when the yard was filled with children. Occurrence: Some small circles of children formed. Within seconds, they had multiplied. In the middle of it all, one could observe – if one came near enough to see – two angry boys in a fierce fight. But it did not last long. The inspecting teacher shuffled his way through the circles, took the boys by ears or neck and brought them to a supposed terrible destiny in front of the Headmaster. Today, they might have been brought to the police station, or to the police stationed at the school. Estrada (1999 and 2001, particularly pp. 650–1) has described this development in two stages of Swedish school history. The old legal director of the Swedish school system stated:

> There is no general requirement to report an offence that has already been committed to the police . . . The schools authority does not

> recommend making a report to the police as a matter of course in
> such a situation . . . It is better the matter to be cleared up on a
> more personal basis in the school, if this is possible – the school
> after all bears a heavy responsibility for the pupils.

And then the new director:

> When something happens, it should be reported at once. One should
> not first decide whether or not it constitutes an offence. That is a
> matter for the police.

These different views are reflected in the heavy increase in the reporting
of 'youth violence' to the police, but then particularly of non-serious
violence. Methods for reporting have changed from visits to the police
station to reports by phone and fax.

1.7 Angry old people

Very old people are often presented as sweet, modest, considerate people.
Life has matured them. Now, close to death, they are grateful for what is
done to them, and kind to those nursing them at the institutions for old
folks. This is the picture, and it is often right. But there are exceptions,
and Malin Åkerström (2000, 2002) has gone into these exceptions.
Some old people bite, hit the nurses, pull their hair, push them towards
walls, create severe bodily harm, and behave in ways that in other settings
certainly would have been called violent. But not in the homes for old
people.

According to Åkerström, a third of those who work at nursing homes
report that they every week are receivers of such behaviour, while similar
acts only are reported in 14 per cent of cases in mental hospitals. Nonetheless, the nurses in the old folks' homes do not call it violence what
here goes on.

Instead, it turns out that the nurses tend to describe what goes on by
de-dramatizing the occurrences. The nurses apply lots of jokes when they
describe events that have taken place. And they apply general ideology
among nurses. The patients are, literally, to be met with patience. In addition comes that the old people's physical aggression does not fall into the
category of violence, they are often clearly confused. And it does not help
to see their acts as some sort of crime. They cannot be punished, and they
are already in an institution supposed to give treatment.

1.8 Recovery from war

Our destiny in modern society is to live among strangers. This is a situation particularly well suited for giving unwanted acts the meaning of being crimes.

The importance of closeness/distance in the creation of meaning is visible in all areas of life. It is particularly important in war – it is easier to see enemy actions as criminal than to see one's own actions in that way. And the dimension closeness/distance is important *after* war. In 1945, when Germany was defeated and five years of military occupation came to an end, Norwegian authorities initiated a fierce penal process directed at those who had collaborated with the occupiers. All members of the Nazi party were defined as having committed a crime, so were also those who had helped the occupiers in various other ways. Executions were used as punishment, the ordinary prisons became too small, old German prison camps were filled with collaborators. During the occupation and immediately after the German surrender, there was no end to public fantasy on death and deportation for the collaborators.

But, as time went on, two tendencies became apparent. First, punishments became less severe. So much so that it became necessary to revise the first sentences. War and occupation came in the background; it made it possible to see some of the collaborators more as ordinary human beings. The other trend was that those charged with economic collaboration with the Germans were given a particularly lenient treatment. Dag Ellingsen (1993) describes the phenomenon. Not all economic collaborators were leniently treated, he says. Those who came before the courts early on got very severe sentences, just as other collaborators. But those with these early sentences were at the same time mostly small fishes, simple cases for prosecution, easily processed in overburdened court systems. The big ones had cases it took a long time to prepare. It might have been entrepreneurs who started improving airports for the Germans in the southern part of Norway before the war had ended in the far north, and who continued their economic collaboration during the five years of occupation. The passing of time in such cases meant in general greater lenience.

In addition, there were other factors. Complicated cases meant endless interrogations by the police, and mobilization of lawyers acting on behalf of the collaborators. These lawyers were not the ordinary defenders of people usually seen as criminals, but experts on civil law, respectable middle and upper class lawyers. And the complications meant many and long days in court by accused persons of a social standing not usually met in penal courts. It became increasingly difficult to see their acts as crime and the actors as criminals. Towards the end of all these processes, a further complication emerged. The country had to be rebuilt. The top echelon of those charged with economic collaboration were exactly those with the best potential to do that job. They owned the big firms, partly developed through their collaboration with the occupiers, but now an asset. It became more and more difficult to see their former acts as 'real' crime and the actors as criminals deserving punishment by the state.

The fate of one man captures much of this. This was *not* a case of economic crime. More serious than money, the man had collaborated at the top level and joined the Nazi cabinet created by Vidkun Quisling. He had acted as Minister of Cultural Affairs, and was sentenced to death. His case came before the Supreme Court. Usually, the accused does not appear there in person. But the accused *can* insist on attending, and this man did. Day after day, he was escorted to the courtroom, this prototype of a civil servant. Tired, pale, with a sad face, a worn suit of a type his judges also once used to wear, a polite voice and vocabulary. As a lawyer by education, he could have been one of them, if not for a fatal belief in a different political system. The Supreme Court changed the death sentence to one of life imprisonment. A participant in the process, whose identity I do not want to reveal, insists that it was the minister's daily appearance in the court that rescued his life. There was no doubt that his acts were criminal according to an interpretation of the law seen as valid at the time, but he came too close to his judges to stand out as so much of a criminal that he had to die.

1.9 Crime as an unlimited natural resource

Crime is in endless supply. Acts with the potentiality of being seen as crimes are like an unlimited natural resource. We can take out a little in the form of crime – or a lot. Acts are not, they become; their meanings are created as they occur. To classify and to evaluate are core activities for human beings. The world comes to us as we constitute it. Crime is thus a product of cultural, social and mental processes. For all acts, including those seen as unwanted, there are dozens of possible alternatives to their understanding: bad, mad, evil, misplaced honour, youth bravado, political heroism – or crime. The 'same' acts can thus be met within several parallel systems as judicial, psychiatric, pedagogical, theological.

But let it be quite clear: I do not say, here or later, that unacceptable acts, completely unacceptable also to me do not exist. I do not deny that some people get bullets into their bodies due to other people's guns. Nor do I deny that some are killed due to other people's cars, that money is taken away from people's drawers or bank accounts without their consent. And I do not deny that I have strong moral objections to most of these acts, try to stop them, and try to prevent them. Nor do I deny that it might be useful to see some of these acts as crime.

I am interested in how meanings are born and are shaped. But that is no immoral position. My world is filled with values, many of which command me to act and re-act. But that does not hinder a keen interest in how acts get their meaning.

With this general perspective, there are some traditional questions in criminology I will *not* ask. Particularly, I will not find it useful asking what is the development in the crime situation. This does not mean that crime statistics are without interest. Such statistics inform on phenomena seen and registered by a particular society as crime and also what happens to those seen as major actors. But crime statistics are themselves social phenomena. They tell what the system sees as crime and bothers to cope with, or has capacity to cope with. Crime statistics are a social fact in dire need for interpretation. This view on crime statistics has consequences. It means that it is not useful to ask if crime is on the increase, stable, or on the decrease. Crime does not exist as a given entity. To measure the variations in the occurrence of a phenomenon that changes its content over time is not among the most tempting of tasks.

I am on this point probably in some disagreement with David Garland (2001) in his book on *The Culture of Control*. I say 'probably' in disagreement. That is because Garland in his interesting book to me is unclear on this point. I am of the impression that he says that crime exists as a phenomenon we can describe as an entity that varies over time and that we can say it is on the increase or decrease. I am also of the impression that he is of the opinion that crime has increased, and that this belief is an important element in his analysis. But he is guarded on this point. I hope his basic position is that we have moved into a social situation where an *impression* is created of a situation of increased crime, and that this impression has all sorts of social consequences.

* * *

This general perspective on crime makes it possible to raise two inter-related central questions:

First, what is behind increases or decreases in acts generally perceived as unwanted or unacceptable? And how is it eventually possible to influence the occurrence of these unwanted acts?

Second, what is it that makes a shifting quota of these unwanted acts to appear as crimes and the actors as criminals? Particularly, under what material, social, cultural and political conditions will crime and criminals appear as the dominant metaphors, the dominant way of seeing the unwanted acts and actors?

This is a liberating perspective. It opens for the general theme of this book: When is enough, enough? Or, as in the title, what is a suitable amount of crime? This question leads naturally into the next: What is a suitable amount of punishment?

2 Monocultures

2.1 On multidimensionality

It is part of our common knowledge that we live in multicultural societies. We have developed from life in simple, homogeneous villages where we were all fairly similar, in bodies as well as in values. But slowly, the globe became one. We were in this process forced to get acquainted with differences. We have experienced a development from living in monocultures to living in multicultures.

This is correct enough, but also completely wrong.

I remember a beautiful, warm summer's day just north of the Arctic Circle. The local ferry was headed towards one of those tiny islands where people can make a living just because they are so close to the fish and whales of that North Sea. A small number of houses sought protection against the wind and ocean behind some cliffs. As we slowly approached the harbour, we observed a man chopping his winter wood. It is a heavy job. He had only shorts on in the summer heat. In a harmonious, rhythmic way he split one piece of wood after another. An ancient Norwegian picture. Man and nature in harmony, an unbroken line from the age of the Vikings. Several children watched him. Soon they would continue the tradition.

Is there more to tell? Only that the man and the kids were all completely black. Even the fishing villages far in the North have lost their homogeneity. And this, of course, is also the case in other parts of Norway, only more so. In my local neighbourhood in Oslo, more than 50 per cent of the pupils in the grammar school have Norwegian as their second language. So, it is completely correct to say that we have moved from mono- to multi-, both with regard to colour and language.

But then comes the next question: Are these observations on colour and language good indicators of multiculturalism? People are different. But that might only be on the outside. Perhaps it is true as stated in progressive books for children: Inside we are similar! My reasoning in what follows is that these progressive books might be right. But then, deplorably right. Back in history we were sometimes, but not always, multicultural. It is now that we are solidly similar. Similar in what we find worth striving for.

*   *   *

To come closer to this problem, we might move to another analytical level. Instead of asking if *individuals* are different from each other, we might ask if the major *institutions* are different from each other. With *institutions* I have in mind the ordering of the major elements of societies. Institutions are clusters of central activities – with their values, norms and behaviour. It is possible to divide them into a large number of different institutions, or to gather the many into a few, more abstract categories. Dag Østerberg (1991) applies a classification of four major categories. In the first, we find *production* of material necessities and *exchange relationships* based on money, with goal-rationality as the dominant thought-pattern. Another category contains *reproduction*, with care and consideration for others as central. A third institution contains activities around *power and politics*, and in a fourth we find institutions for the *elaboration of symbols and understanding*, at the level of daily life or systematized within education, science and art.

And then to an important question: We are in sociology used to looking at institutions, or major groupings among them, as basically different. It is just these differences that make it possible to differentiate them, give them different names, compare their distinctive features and their mutual strength. Pluralism is often our intuitive picture in such an analysis.

But it is also possible to have another picture. It is possible to have a picture where the one institution expands, invades the other institutions, consumes them. This is a picture of a sort of institutional imperialism where the one institution gains complete domination, where all is determined from this institution, and/or where important parts of most or all other institutions become colonized.

And where are we in this picture?

2.2 The great-aunts

I have vivid childhood memories from time spent with three great-aunts. Maria Hansine was born in 1852, Sara in 1854 and Anna in 1859. They came from a dynasty of priests, an important class of their time, but with costs attached. They had high status, but little money to live on according to the standards of their class. Little money meant reduced possibilities for marriage and children. Males could not propose on nothing – and the females in that situation were without a dowry as an incentive. In addition came the inconvenience for these females that some suitable males sneaked off and married particularly attractive ones from the lower classes. This created a deficit of eligible males for the girls from the dynasty. Marie and Sara never married. Anna did at a rather mature age, remained childless, and moved in with the two sisters as soon as her husband died. But my great-uncles were also strictly controlled by the destiny of their sisters. They were supposed to support them, which blocked attempts for their own marriages. There were four brothers. The oldest escaped to another country while his sisters were small and still provided for by their parents. Here he created a family. The two next in age were just a bit older than their three sisters. They remained unmarried their whole life. There was some talk about great-uncle Gerhardt and a lady when once he had worked as a house teacher up in the valleys, but it could never materialize. The sisters owned nothing. They had no paid work, of course not. They lived in other people's houses and brought up other families' children. Uncle Gerhardt provided for the bare necessities. The fourth among the boys, my grandfather, was rescued for reproduction by being the youngest in the family, which meant that the sisters were taken care of by his two elder brothers long before he came of age. The three sisters were very poor. I learned later that for a long period they shared one winter coat. It troubled them that each of them could go to church only every third winter Sunday. But their trouble lay more in their relation to God than to neighbours. They lived at a time where one might be poor, but proud. Or brilliant, but materially living in misery. Or an essential family member, but without any personal income. Remarks heard at funerals might be that she was such a bright woman, one with clever advice on how to manage complicated social or material situations. Or, maybe it would be said that she was always so kind, she never kept much for herself. She lived according to the saying: Nothing can come into a closed hand. Or an honest soul has left us, or, she never harmed a flea.

My point is not a nostalgic one. I do not need to evaluate whether the life of my great-aunts and great-uncles was better or worse than my own or my grandchildren's life seems to be. My point is simply that their life illustrates a multi-institutional situation. They praised God, but consumed, behind curtains, their aquavit 'to prevent colds'. They were fond of books, but that fondness was not for a living. They were proud of the family, but that also within limits.[1] They worked all their lives in other people's families, but earned next to nothing, measured in money. That troubled their lives, but not their self-respect. They were haunted by poverty, but died – as far as I can ascertain – with a feeling that they had lived dignified lives. They lived in an age where one single institution was not in total control of their lives, even though the religious one probably meant most to them. Basically, they lived a life under institutional pluralism.

2.3 Development as imperialism

A dominant idea in our culture is to go out and shape all societies into our picture. So also with modernity.

It was in 1949 that Harry Truman launched the campaign for fighting underdevelopment, changing the globe into one of a family of highly industrialized nations. The poor of the Third World were to be rescued from their underdevelopment and poverty. It was a forceful ideology, presuming that the good life was the one lived according to the standards dominated by economic rationality.

But it was at the same time an idea which meant that all nations ought to develop into our model with our simplified goal structure. The concept *underdevelopment* later vanished. Instead came the term *developing countries*; it sounds more optimistic, as if they are underway. The correct designation of today is *Countries of the Third World*. But the realities are the same. Countries of the Third World are to be helped up to our level; their third class wagons are to be rebuilt, to be like ours of the first class. But to get this done, these countries have to change one essential feature: From being multi-institutional, they have to become mono-institutional. They will then, *as nations*, be able to work themselves out of their situation of international dependency. At least, that is the dream. They will not – as states – have to beg for help and assistance from the highly industrialized countries. But some of their citizens will have to beg for help, from the very states that now have come (or have been promised soon to come) out of their national dependency. In this process, national dependency is exchanged for *individual* dependency. Or, in another picture: Countries of the Third World were, in all their underdevelopment, often organized in ways with a place for all people, a need for all hands. As these societies now move into the category of nations of producers and consumers, a great number of their inhabitants come into the situation where they lose full participation in the activities seen as the only important ones: the activities of production and consumption.

Ivan Illich (1992, p. 90) says:

> Well into the industrial age, for most people living in subsistence
> cultures, life was still predicated on the recognition of limits that

just could not be transgressed. Life was bounded within the realm of immutable necessities. The soil yielded only known crops; the trip to the market took three days; the son could infer from the father what his future would be . . . needs, meaning necessities, had to be endured . . . In a moral economy of subsistence, the existence of desires is taken as much for granted as the certainty that they could not be stilled.

One lived the life that was. One had wishes, but then in the form of hope, not as needs based on rights. The human being is, in the perspective of Illich, transformed from *Homo sapiens* (the wise or tasteful human) into *Homo miserabilis*.

Seen like this, the idea of development is an imperialistic idea. Imperialistic in the arrogance of the highly developed nations saying: We are helping you to be as *we* are. And imperialistic in the fact that the help consists of encouragement and/or coercion to force these nations from a multi-institutional organization into a mono-institutional one by letting ideas and values from one single, dominant institution colonize the others.

2.4 The rewards of labour

I remember, with strong colours and emotions, the day in my life I came to know I had been appointed to a permanent job at the University. Tenure, a job for life. In a whole life spent in research I have had the fortune never ever to have had to do anything because it would give me money. It has been the other way around. I have received money that enabled me to do what I am so fond of doing.

I am far from alone in living this type of privileged life in my country. Similarly privileged, maybe more so, are certain people usually called mentally retarded. I prefer to call them extraordinary. They, and some supposedly ordinary people, live in six villages in various parts of Norway. The same types of villages can be found in several countries in Europe, particularly in Great Britain and Germany.

One essential feature of the inner life of these villages is that they have broken the connection between work and money. All villagers work, but one of the basic features of these villages is that money is not used as a reward. Simply: all money is put into one hat, and used according to needs, but money is not used *as a reward*.

In the official budget, terms such as teacher, nurse, doctor and farmer are used. But these terms have limited meaning inside the village. And most importantly, the income from these positions will never reach the holders of these positions. All money from the state and the municipalities, and also all income from the sales of vegetables or of pottery from the village are placed in a joint account for the whole village.

But the villagers are cared for, independently of their condition. They have a room in a house with very extraordinary people – and with some people not extraordinary in any way other than that they prefer to live in villages like this. They all have access to the usual comforts of modern life: healthy food, a car if necessary for those who can drive or a seat in one for those who cannot, or a vacation trip to Greece with others from the village, or to a music festival in St Petersburg.

Students listen in disbelief if I tell about the joint account, all money in one hat, and from that one, all can use according to need. It cannot be possible. It will lead to abuse, or to endless internal quarrels on how to use the money. My answer is: Make an attempt to discuss this matter with very old workers. So old that they do not talk about social security, but *sykekasse*, literally the little box where they all regularly put a fraction of their salary during those weeks they had the good luck to receive a salary. It was from this box they received some money if the body could not endure more. The definition of an ailing body was up to the worker. The problem with the money in the box was not abuse, but the opposite – under use. So also in the village. The experience of joint destiny promotes Spartan living. The level of consumption is a consequence of the organization of the social system. Living in grand systems with supposed leaks at both ends, one type of morality is mobilized. Living in small systems where it is obvious that one's behaviour has direct consequences for everybody else, quite another morality might become mobilized.

Money in the common hat makes it easier to break the connection between work and money. I have never, ever, heard anybody in the villages mention money as an incentive for taking on a task. The reason for work is the need for having work done. Everybody works. Some with enthusiasm, others with considerable ability to take it easy. But money, or the lack of it, is never mentioned as a reason for the activity. Cows have to be milked, their tails kept away from the milk bucket – sometimes an important task – weeds removed, dinner prepared, the lame moved by the blind and the blind directed by the lame. Money is a necessity in relation to the external world, but irrelevant internally. This has immediate consequences for the evaluation of the activities. The reward from the work is the work. In English, in contrast to Norwegian, one has the possibility of differentiating between the two concepts 'labour' and 'work'. Labour is the heavy burden; the word is historically related to torture. Work has an air of accomplishment; it is close to creation, creating a work of art! To this act of creating, money is a threat. The work does not become a reward in itself. It becomes a tool for something else, and thereby converted into labour.

With reduced importance given to money and consumption, room is given for other activities. Vidaråsen is the name of the major village in the system. Here, there are numerous ordinary buildings – family houses, craft shops, a farm – and three major, public buildings. The greatest is the Hall. Here, in a village of 160 people, we find the greatest concert and theatre hall in the county. Musicians love to come here for performances. The next major building is what I call the 'Tent', used for religious functions, but also for lectures and other cultural activities. And then the third building, just finished, a centre for giving help to people in need of an extraordinary amount or some special type of care. Three buildings, all raised by money from that hat, three symbols of institutions of central importance in the village: culture, religion and care. Together with work, they are central elements in this type of village life. It allows for a multiplicity of life activities. It opens, literally, a place for all.

But do not let us romanticize: Small, tightly knit societies such as these, where people are mutually dependent, such societies are also filled with internal conflicts. I have in another connection (Christie 1973) published a small article with the title 'A Living Society is a Quarrelling Society'. This statement is a suitable description of some of the realities of the villages as well.

I have for many years been connected to these villages and also described them in a little book titled *Beyond Loneliness and Institutions* (1987). Two years ago, I was asked to write a new preface to an Italian translation and did so. But since such a long time had gone by since the first edition, the editor asked me to describe how the villages had developed from the time I had made my first observation by living there some 15 years back. And I felt some sort of embarrassment. Actually, not much had happened. It had been a period of stability, not of change.

But why should that be an embarrassment? Why is it so that non-change is more difficult to describe than change? I think it is because non-development is against the spirit of the time and therefore so easily interpreted as a defect. Vidaråsen and the other villages represent a type of life which has not succumbed to the pressure of development. They have refused to modernize. They have analysed the values of the old societies, made themselves aware of them, and reorganized life in accordance with these values.

So, this is the problem when describing later developments. Nothing much has happened since the first edition. And why should it? Village life has a slow rhythm: birth, ageing, death – and the arrival of some newcomers for a year or for life. Some new buildings, some restoration of old ones, but mostly life has continued; it has been village life as usual.

But then comes the next and challenging question: How is this possible? How to explain non-development in a world filled with belief in progress?

I have no certain answers, but some suggestions. First comes the emphasis on the villagers as the reference point for all major activities in the villages. Several of those living there have trouble walking, which limits the size of the area villages can grow. Unwillingness to accept bureaucratic hierarchies has the same effect. Such forms of organization are difficult to prevent if size is increased. The elimination of money as an incentive is also a factor. There is nothing to gain by building big or modern. On the contrary, development might easily be seen as a threat against life qualities – more people to relate to, less time for close contacts.

But still, many of those living in the villages have grown up in 'normal society'. They have been socialized to the goal of progress; they have been trained to get a job, a family, advance socially as well as economically, perhaps to create a firm for themselves – all the usual signs of success. Why do they stay on? Why do they not change the villages into modern nursing homes of one sort or another?

I believe the major reason is that the villages are filled with *alternative* challenges. If you live close to a human without ordinary language, it is an enormous victory if you one day manage to understand the body language of that person and later even advance in that understanding. If a person who has never walked alone between two houses one day per-forms such an act of heroism, it is an act that fills much of the day with joy. In addition come all the other social rewards connected with ghetto life. There are many stabilizers in village life.

But still, it might have gone wrong. The villages might have been destroyed by their economic situation. Not by lack of money, but because of their surplus!

I have already mentioned their basic arrangement of having all money in one hat. What I now need to mention is that this principle gives the villages the possibility to become relatively affluent social systems. The villages receive less money from the Norwegian state than other systems with as many persons with extraordinary difficulties would have received. But people living here have nearly no private economy. The village is their home. They do not have to buy houses, cars, insurance. Therefore, much of the money remains in the hat for all. And from that hat it is used for renovating houses, for new horses, for buying more land, or for building a new hall for celebrating, or building new houses for new villagers. And here is the threat. The money might have led to an over expansion, to additional rewards for particularly deserving villagers – rewards which might have threatened the egalitarian standards inside the village, or to a general living standard so high above the usual for Norway that trouble might have followed. The very stability of the villages might have been endangered, not because of too little money, but because of too much.

This problem has been solved by generosity.

The most remarkable thing that has happened since I made my first observations has been an enormous expansion of the village movement in Eastern Europe. Four new villages have been established, one in Russia, one in Estonia, one in Poland and, most recently, one in Lithuania. All of them have received major assistance from the Norwegian villages in the form of money, buildings, equipment and personnel. Observing this development, I was initially hesitant and feared that the Norwegian villages had over-stretched themselves. Money and manpower were needed inside the Norwegian villages; it was dangerous to send it all to the East.

I was wrong. I should have remembered the institution of potlatch. Or I should have remembered other cases described by social anthropologists, cases where the surplus was destroyed, sent away or redistributed so that the basic structure of the tribe or the community was not changed or destroyed. Help given to create villages in Eastern Europe has enabled villages in Norway to preserve their identity. The entrepreneurial drive gained a non-destructive outlet. The surplus has been used for good purposes. It has been for development, but then development in the sense of more villages, more examples of alternative ways of living. And this in nations where these alternatives are highly needed in competition with the ordinary Westernized ideas now penetrating the East with their message of the blessings of economic competition and development.

2.5 How to get children to stop building

Children are nearly always active children. They feed their dolls and fight their wars, they build castles from cartons or palaces in sand. They do it for fun, create for nothing except the process itself. The important and difficult question is why so many let these activities come to an end, why they stop creating.

Because it is such a strenuous activity?

Look at youngsters building some sort of a cottage up in a tree. Or look at it in fantasy if there are no youngsters around. Such youngsters can carry on from early morning to late at night, drag planks to the place, saw, hammer, hit the nails and hurt their fingers. This can continue over days, weeks, until the construction stands there and plans for a new project slowly emerge.

We are born as creators. But the work can get away from us in several ways. The most dangerous is salary. It takes attention away from the work. No longer is what one does central, but what one earns from it. Work becomes a means for something else, and the activity becomes what the Germans would call *uneigentlich* – it is no longer an activity to create something, but an activity to accomplish something different, something in addition to the creation: the monetary reward. Give the kids money for building huts in the trees, and the activity will soon come to an end.

By removing the relation between work and salary, something else is also removed: the peculiar belief that people have salaries as deserved. Deserved, or even most deserved, and therefore the highest salary? Because one is the best dollmaker in the town or in the country? Because dolls are more asked for than rocking horses? Because one was born into a family of dollmakers? Because one had sufficient power and/or was ruthless enough to create a monopoly of doll production? Where the reward of the work is the work, it becomes apparent that monetary differences in ordinary society have so many other reasons than the work itself.

Money to the kids could soon bring their building activities to a stop. In addition, I know of only one other effective method to stop, even prevent, their building activity. That is if I instructed them on how to do it. If I immediately grabbed the hammer, let them carefully look while I demonstrated, and then arranged a little course in cottage building with a final exam and certification of those found good enough to climb trees. At the level of 'the hut in the trees', the idea is absurd. At the social level, this is exactly how we arrange things – and thereafter start wondering why so many children gradually turn so passive.

2.6 Capital

We know that George Simmel (e.g. 1990, p. 404) was right. Money is the enemy of primary relations: 'Money makes it possible for us to buy ourselves not only out of bonds with others but also out of those that stem from our own possessions.' Money becomes itself a symbol of strangeness. If I ask a close friend to help me move my furniture from one house to another, and then at the end of a long day of moving ask him to send me a bill, he will either take it as a joke or be seriously hurt. Offering him money will, if done seriously, imply telling him that 'we are not friends' (Gezelius 2002, p. 241).

Some time back, I asked a group of students for their thoughts when I mentioned the word 'capital'. Nearly all, and few with any hesitation, said: 'Money'. I had the day before gone to the *Oxford English Dictionary*, and was well prepared to state that money was mentioned only as definition number eight in that well of knowledge. Top of a column, heads, major city, major building – these are closer to the original meaning. It says a lot about our time that money has taken the place of heads.

In the very old cities, the cathedrals were the landmarks, with royal palaces as a close number two. Later came universities and schools. In my neighbourhood, the school is still the largest among buildings. What a monument to the importance of the institution of education it must have been 110 years back in time, a five-floor structure with a metal tower shaped like a Bismarck-helmet at the top. Palaces for God, palaces for kings, palaces for knowledge and education. And now, in modern cities, these are all overshadowed by skyscrapers and shopping centres; palaces for trade and money. The target of September 11th was not a random choice.

2.7 The new cathedral

It happened in Canada. As the high point of triviality, I wanted to buy some underwear and left my quarters to find it. It can be cold in Canada, and several cities have rebuilt their city centres so that shoppers of all sorts can move indoors from building to building. At the second floor level are built small closed-in bridges to help prospective customers cross the streets and, undisturbed by wind and snow, continue their hunt for goods. The streets below are for cars and less dressed-up persons – those that discreetly are denied access to public rooms, which are not public any more.

Soon I had lost my way in this labyrinth of commodities. Furs to the left, scarves straight ahead, and then a bridge, and where now is the hotel, and then this damned underwear? Not until I had passed some skiing equipment, gone through an opening in a wall, and then suddenly, I was there. In the cathedral. An Asiatic couple and myself arrived at exactly the same time. We just gaped. I had not seen anything like this since Rome. The enormous headroom, the dome, the stained glass. We had landed in a sort of gallery. Deep down, I could dimly see the floor. Dimly? Not quite, I got a glimpse of my most important concern: a department for male underwear.

It was to one of the largest department stores in Canada that I had come.

* * *

Our past does provide numerous examples of mono-institutional epochs, situations where certain institutions gained close to an absolute dominance. It might have been the family which had the power, societies where kinship position determined most of people's lives – as distribution of property and political loyalties. Or it might have been the church that dominated, where canon law was the ultimate source for all sorts of legal decisions, where kings and queens bowed to the authority of the archbishops, and where the Bible was seen as lending authority to the husband's absolute rule within the family. Or we can find examples where the military dominated everything, where the warrior was the central role model for the aristocracy and where their heroic war adventures ruined nations. These are all cases of institutional imperialism where one institution colonizes most of the others.

2.8 On the move

The old landowners had a problem. They had their roots in their property. Some liked to live there, and became respected figures in their neighbourhoods. Others might have been more exploitative, but even these had to invest in social ties. They were dependent on labour, and on a minimum of trust and loyalty in local neighbourhoods. At least this was the case if they did not have total power as slave owners. So also with those who owned factories, or some sort of business. Without a minimum of decency, barns might mysteriously burn, machinery might come to unexpected stops, or no one would join them on that windy night they had to cross the fjord to fetch the doctor.

The new types of owners, the money movers, are in a dramatically different, and historically completely unique, situation. Their property has no weight. It moves by a touch of a button. And they are free to move with their property. They are the new vagabonds, well equipped for the voyage to those destinations which at any time are seen as the most helpful for the preservation or the growth of their money. For this, they have their own information systems, most of course through informal networks, but also through various journals. One of them, *International Living*, advertises continually cheap property all over the world, particularly in countries hit by natural or political disasters where the price of house and property are at the very bottom. The Argentine has been a dream for cheap bargains in spring 2003, but hurry up, conditions might normalize. Nicaraguan bargains are still available, and then, of course, there is continuous information about tax havens. The journal brought me to Dr W. G. Hill in *The Passport Report*, 11th edition from 1997. We read:

Why entrust your life and your freedom to any government? With only one passport you are accountable to politicians who can regard you as an expendable resource. You can be monitored, labelled and contained. But this need not be the case. With two or more passports, you need not 'belong' to any country. You are your own jurisdiction. Your personal and financial independence can be preserved. Your mobility is ensured.

. . .

This is not to suggest that you need to breach any law to obtain your second travel document. Far from it. W. G. Hill would never advise anything of the kind. What he can do is to tell you how to legally obtain documents in your own name . . . In many situations there is no residence requirement. In a few places there is not even any need to ever visit.

2.9 A mono-institutional society

We are not in the time of my great-aunts. We are in a mono-institutional situation, in a situation of institutional imperialism, but this time by the swelling of the institution of production, trade and exchange of money.

Buildings are symbols of institutional hegemony. But so is also what happens inside these buildings, particularly how life is organized. Ideals from the area of economy and production have clearly invaded the neighbouring institutions. Money is the crowbar; activities are to be evaluated according to their profit, and profit is measured in money according to the principle of most to those supposedly having the highest productivity. It seems obvious. But if one is not born into the idea, it is of course far from obvious that activities outside of the institution of production and trade should be rewarded in this way.

Most money for the best mother? No, here we put on some brakes. But most money for the most valuable scientist? Here some of the brakes are gone. And even within the institution of religion, fights about money become visible. Norway has a 'state church'. Some time back the trade union for priests threatened to call a strike to increase the general salary level for its members. But it has not gone as far as claiming most money for those particular individuals seen as the 'best' preachers, those attracting the biggest congregations. But leading bishops receive higher salaries than ordinary bishops, and priests with large congregations more than those with small. And Members of Parliament, usually so fond of the idea of salaries according to market value, still seem to be hesitant in deciding that backbenchers ought to get lower salaries than frontbenchers. But in May 2003, a parliamentary commission in my country proposed an increased salary for the President of Parliament, and also for the chairpersons of all the parliamentary committees.

The hegemony of market thinking is so clearly established in our time that in a way it has become invisible. It becomes an obvious part of life. How could it be otherwise? To be able to question the obvious, let us draw some slightly less respectable parallels.

2.10 A total solution

To understand a phenomenon, it is useful to compare. We have already described a situation where one institution has penetrated all of the other major institutions. What is similar to this? Let us for a moment look into the phenomenon of totalitarianism.

The origin of that word is not quite clear. Klein (1971) suggests in his etymological dictionary that the concept totalitarianism is related to *towetos* – crammed fully – which again is related to *tumere* – to swell, as in cancer. So far, this is not too distant from developments in the market economy. But more is usually said about totalitarian societies.

Carl Friedrich, quoted here in Linz (1975, pp. 187–9), has this definition of totalitarian regimes:

(1) a totalist ideology;
(2) a single party committed to this ideology and usually led by one man, the dictator;
(3) a fully developed secret police and three kinds of monopoly or more precisely monopolistic control, namely, that of (a) mass communications, (b) operational weapons, and (c) all organizations including economic ones, thus involving a centrally planned economy.

Bernt Hagtvet (1981, pp. 285–6) says:

Totalitarian states represent an attempt to suspend or weaken the structural differentiation usually found in modern states. In totalitarian dictatorships we find that economy, cultural life, family, the legal apparatus and all other subsystems have only limited autonomy compared to the political system.

Measured against totalitarian *dictatorships*, it does not seem sensible to say that we, due to the enormous dominance of the market economy, live in a totalitarian regime. But if we do not insist that dictatorship is a necessity for totalitarian phenomenon to appear, then the situation changes. If we stick to the history of the concept, *tumere* – to swell – it is not entirely unreasonable to pay attention to totalitarian features attached to our present system. Maybe the tradition of looking at totalitarian regimes as the product of dictators prevents us from seeing the totalitarian character of our present existence.

* * *

My contention is that we in recent society have moved in the direction of the old situation with one totally dominating institution penetrating most of the other institutions. Modernity has production and consumption as its dominant centre. Not according to the ideas of one man, or according to one single master plan, even though many of the international activities to increase international trade are close to having that character. No dictator says that money and consumption are the goals in life. But it is told. Not by the great shows – the big parades, the military music. Our time is the time of the beautiful people – the exposure of how they live, how they become what they are. What a shame not to succeed. In the sale of its message, the market industry of today is probably considerably more efficient than the propaganda apparatus belonging to the old totalitarian dictatorships.

2.11 Costs of a monolithic reward system

We still have some lagoons where alternative values are listened to, some secret gardens, some monasteries, some academies, some bohemian circles, some opposing youth cultures. But the dominant ideas are to be found within the economic institution with production, monetary gain and consumption at the centre.

Such societies, with their highly simplified reward systems, are faced with certain built-in problems. In multi-institutional societies, there are institutions where the theme of monetary reward does not enter the picture. One plays for the sake of playing, walks to the river for the sake of the walk, joins friends or kin for the sake of joining. With the introduction of money into an increasing number of activities, one is confronted with a situation offering a diminished availability of the types of activities that represent a reward in themselves. In addition, if money, eventually the use of money, becomes the goal of all activities, life becomes sad and empty for those without. There are so few other arenas left. Lack of money becomes a clear indicator that life has been a failure.

A person I know reasonably well said at the age of 13: I wish I would never grow any older. Probably she expressed that the life of the grown-ups was not particularly enticing. A saying goes that in the old days, there were no alternatives. People were in the heavy labour behind the plough or in the household, knowing that their life would be as that of their forefathers and foremothers. While we are free to create our own destiny. But it is, of course, also possible to come to the opposite conclusion: The old ones had many tasks besides those behind the plough and their domestic chores, while our lives are restricted in the sense that earning money and spending it is such an overwhelming goal for all activities. When it comes to the goals in life, we live in a monolith, kept there as in granite.

Seen from the point of view of economic rationality, there is no great need for manpower or womanpower in highly industrialized societies. What most do well, the machines, or workers from less industrialized countries, can do better. Redundancy is the destiny of a considerable number among us – among the young, the old, the sick, the less qualified, those with the wrong colour, those with the wrong culture. For a large number of these, paid work is just a distant dream. So is also their role as consumers based on money earned in the biblical manner of sweat. Humans in this situation might get into deep trouble. So also society with them.

2.12 Shining São Paulo

Not long ago I paid a visit to Brazil. São Paulo is the economic centre of the country, a hectic city of unbelievable wealth. As always in new settings, it took some time to understand the meaning of the messages. I was soon confronted with two statements and one observation:

1   Even on cold days, I always drive with the windows closed and therefore with the air conditioning on, said one lady. What a lack of concern for the preservation of energy, was my reflection.
2   I never stop for red lights during the night, was another statement. What an anti-social driver, was my thought.
3   And then the observation: A common phenomenon in poor countries is the gathering of youngsters around all major street crossings, offering coffee, lemonade, newspapers and the cleaning of car windows. But not so in São Paulo.

The common denominator: The fear of crime. Air conditioning had to be used in the cars because windows had to remain closed from fear of robberies. To stop at crossings was seen as dangerous, therefore one crossed on red. And because of closed windows and no stopping, there were no possibilities for service and sales.

A colleague interviewed me for a legal journal. She was an activist for prisoners' rights. She mentioned, casually, that she had been robbed eight times during recent years. A friend of hers, a lecturer in criminology, was in another type of turmoil just days before I met her. She had a car, but an old one, without air conditioning. So, to survive the heat, she drove with open windows. The traffic was heavy and came to a stop. An arm with a razor blade came through the window touching her throat. The robber – it was a woman – demanded her money. My informant, the criminologist, was tired and hot and hungry and on her way home to feed the kids. Enough was enough, no more robbing today, she said and put the car in motion. The woman with the razor blade retreated and went away – shaking her head. Highly undeserved, she had met a victim without manners.

I went to the local police station the day after. It was a tiny building next to a large international hotel with single rooms and double rooms, well suited for accommodating visitors. In the police cell, 70 men shared one room. There was not space for all to sit down at the same time. The two showers could not be used during daytime since prisoners were standing there to relieve the pressure in the main room. The temperature, the odour, the congestion, the waving of arms through the bars – Dante might have had trouble in believing his eyes.

Back in the city; electrical fences everywhere and watchmen with guns outside most large buildings. One keeps what one has, and with all means available. Up in the hills, in comfortable distance from the apartment palaces, some lights could be seen. These lights came from the barrios, the poor people's self-made houses and neighbourhoods.

Brazil is not Scandinavia, but maybe Scandinavia becomes a bit more Brazil each time we install an extra lock?

Once a year in Norway a huge activity is organized to collect money. It is for some good purpose at the top of the social agenda – for refugees, for Save the Children, for the fight against AIDS, or against other sorts of misery. Newspapers, radio and TV build up enthusiasm for the good cause, and thousands of collectors move from door to door to collect the money. Recently, some of the veteran collectors were interviewed over radio. It was more heavy work now, they said. Not because people gave less money when contact was established, but because it was so difficult to establish that very contact. In the old days, you might enter the apartment block and walk from door to door inside the building. Today, the collectors do not get access to the buildings without knowing someone there. The main entrances to the blocks are nearly always locked these days. The money collectors may ring the bell, but doors are not necessarily opened. Dangers might lurk outside. The neighbours have a responsibility for each other.

2.13 Crime-free territories

My home is my castle. In that castle, one might have a room for oneself, a room where it is possible to be completely private.

Private?

The word has Latin roots. *Privare*, to deprive, the Roman concept for the fate of being cut off from the other, removed from the social, split off from the important, departed from it.

And again we are on home ground. The apartment, yes, exactly, where one is kept apart, away from everywhere else. I have been invited home to people with several locks on their doors and in addition two rods of steel across the doors. It took much time to enter, even for the owner. In some houses, there might be locks on the windows with alarms attached, often with direct lines to the police or the security guards. If such houses are up for sale, it is often because those living there want to move to bigger and better guarded apartment blocks.

The Latin tradition is *la concierge*, that kind but watchful woman. Lately she has changed, first by becoming a man, then a man with a gun, who eventually is moved into a small armed tower with television equipment permitting him to watch the whole compound. A circle of safety is drawn around the whole building. But why only around the building? The entire neighbourhood could be fenced in. Gilded cities, paradises for those with much to lose. They grow up now, in all Western countries. Guards at the entrance see to it that only those with valid reasons and the best of credentials gain access.

A problem remains in the centre of cities, in the public rooms, areas supposed to be for all. Here, more dubious characters might appear. One solution has been to give that type of room semi-private status. The sober bum cannot be denied access to major streets, but when city malls belong to someone, the control is simplified. As pointed out by Bottoms and Wiles (1992), this type of control makes it possible to keep unwanted people away. Skid row people are discreetly, or not so discreetly, told to keep off. Other possibilities are also open. Representative quarters can be fenced off as in Los Angeles, with highways between them and the slum areas near by. Benches can be constructed to make them useless for sleep, and also so that the temptation to remain seated is minimized. At the main railway station in Copenhagen, all benches have been removed, and in addition it is now forbidden to sit down on the floor in the big hall.

When cars came to New York, this was seen as a big hygienic improvement. In earlier days, boots were needed for walking along Fifth Avenue due to manure from horses and pigs. Then cars took priority. The town had to be rebuilt. The horse manure disappeared, and pigpens became more valuable as ground for buildings than for animals. And progress continues these days, now under the banners of criminologists in wars against all those who peculiarly enough seem to prefer living in neighbourhoods where windows are broken. It is easier to stem a brook than a river, easier to stem a river than a flood, and obviously simpler to arrest a person who cheats on the subway than one who later might develop into committing more serious acts.

* * *

What happens to the locks on doors, to the gilded cities, and with those living in the midst of broken windows – this is just in miniature what whole states are doing these days. The rich protect their property by hiding behind walls. So do also the rich states, to keep citizens from the poor states out of their territories. The Scheengen Agreement and other arrangements create whole states as gilded territories.

3 The use-value of crime

3.1 No room for crime

Sometimes it is easier to understand the conditions that create a phenomenon when the conditions are not there. So also with crime.

I passed from child to man in a period when my country was occupied by German forces. At the personal level, I remember those years as easy years. No close relatives or friends were killed, tortured, or physically harmed as a result of war circumstances. We belonged to the national majority, united in negative attitudes towards the occupiers and with an intense despising directed towards the collaborators. Such is life with enemies in the house. It is a life of white and black, angels and devils. In the streetcars, there were posters instructing the passengers that it was an offence to remain standing if there were an empty seat beside a seated German soldier. There were also posters announcing the death penalty for belonging to the resistance movement. All radios were confiscated, TV had not yet arrived, only a few German-friendly newspapers were available, no journals, no theatres, no movies. All athletic arrangements were prohibited, most teachers were for a period arrested and sent to the north of Norway due to their unwillingness to join the Nazi-dominated trade union, no public meetings were held, except those for and by the collaborators. Nonetheless, most of my memories of war are of peace.

It was a time filled with social life.

I was too young to participate in resistance activities and so also were my friends. What remained, seen from the perspective of distant memories, was reading books and a most intense life with other youngsters. We met in homes or at street corners. Autumn evenings, completely dark, no lamp posts, no light from windows, this to prevent British aeroplanes from finding their way. Encounters for endless hours, and then walks back home, in groups, or alone.

Scared during these walks? It never occurred to me, and I think I can include friends of both sexes, and also parents, who saw us leave in the completely darkened evenings. They never admonished: Be careful! There was nothing to fear. German soldiers were monsters by definition but disciplined to the extreme in their daily practices. Crime was no reality. We never thought about it, never talked about it. We talked about all the usual things of daily life, mostly, of course, of love and lust and the end of the war. I cannot remember any discussion about traditional crime, nor of the crime situation in general. Perhaps there is no room left for such a subject during war conditions. The enemy is the criminal, his acts are the crimes. There is no room for more.

* * *

Those days are long since gone in my country. Perhaps that is one of the reasons I feel so much at home in Finland – a country where there still are so many burning themes to disagree on that it is difficult for crime to reach the forefront.

3.2 Where the large conflicts reigned

Tammerfors is the Manchester of Finland, a town of heavy industry, a stronghold for Labour. I arrived there some years back and found the citizens in the middle of a fierce struggle. General Mannerheim was at the centre of it. Mannerheim is a hero of Finland. Major streets have his name. His monument can be found everywhere. Mannerheim on horse-back, Mannerheim on foot, Mannerheim in uniform, ready for war. He gave fame and pride to Finland during the Winter War against the USSR in 1939, and in the Continuation War of 1940–44. So, all towns with self-confidence wanted his monument.

But not Tammerfors.

Mannerheim had a history. A fierce civil war took place in Finland in 1918. The revolution in Russia had spread to Finland. Tammerfors was the stronghold for the Reds. But Mannerheim, he was the general for the Whites. The Whites moved slowly towards Tammerfors. The fight was fierce. Rumours spread that no prisoners were spared. The rumours proved true for some periods of time. The historian Heikki Ylikangas (1995) has revealed what occurred. In the end, Tammerfors fell. Thousands of Reds were killed on the spot or in prison camps during the years that followed.[1]

And now a city council, a new one with distance in time from the civil war, wanted to raise a monument to Mannerheim, the general of the enemies. A compromise was later made. Tammerfors got its monument. It was placed somewhere in the surrounding forest.

What I try to convey is that Finland is, or at least was, a country of intense internal conflicts. It is just recently that the civil war has surfaced as a theme in the public debate. Now it is discussed whether a truth commission should be established. But the deep conflicts have always been felt. Tourist brochures tell of forests and lakes and saunas. This is all true, and well worth a visit. But crossing what is called 'The Long Bridge' in Helsinki, I was reminded by my Finnish companion that this bridge was the last holdout of the machine guns defending what was once the capital of the Reds.

Down at the harbour I marvelled at the beautiful house where one of the last Russian governors in town had his residence. A Finnish patriot shot him. From small boats along the pier, I bought vegetables from Swedish-speaking farmers – they have lived in the vicinity since Finland was captured and made a part of Sweden. On my way back to the town centre, I asked for directions in my best Swedish, but the Finn I met just turned away. Probably he believed me to belong to the Swedish minority in the country, the former occupiers, a large portion of them still upper class. His opinion would probably have been that I ought to have approached him in Finnish, a language I was supposed to have learned in school if I were a Swedish Finn. If I had revealed that I was a Norwegian, and therefore could not be expected to know his language, he would certainly have answered politely, in Swedish if he had mastered it, or in English or in body language. Anyhow, I found my way to an old friend who had just had a baby. She had given the newborn the name Karelia, which is the name of an important part of Finland lost to Russia after World War II.

Not only the lakes, the saunas, and the friendships made Finland the best country in the North. Its long history of conflict also contributed. But recently there are indications that this is about to change. Finland is becoming closer to the core countries in the European community, with their mono-institutional monotony. But just a few years ago, I was again and again struck by the intensity of their cultural and political life. In Finland discussions raged about life, and the not too distant death. They lived with their history of cleavages, and continued with more recent ones. They had had their experience with a sprinkling of fascism in the thirties. They had had a strong communist party after the war – radical youths who turned Stalinist instead of Maoist as in the rest of Scandinavia (Suominen 1996). And then – until the dissolution of the USSR – they had experienced desperate attempts to balance the East and the West in their foreign policy. Visiting Finland meant visiting a country where a broad range of serious problems was under constant heated discussion. And then to my major point: This created a situation where crime was not the dominant theme on the agenda. Crime is, of course, always of interest, but here within limits. They kill each other more in Finland than in the other Nordic countries, but discuss it less. The drug panic did not hit Finland until quite recently. Their discussions on how to control what is seen as crime were more sober than in the other Nordic countries.[2] Until recently, Finland was a sort of negative case, one that confirmed that crime will not dominate the public discourse when so much else matters. The intense interest in the issue of crime as we find it elsewhere might be related to the lack of other issues seen as relevant and important. The war in Iraq will probably for a short period have reduced the interest in more conventional crime in most Western countries.

3.3 The weak state

The situation for most national states has obviously been one of diminished power. If the states do not behave according to the wishes of Big Capital, that capital will just move to another country. So also can Little Capital. There is always a heaven on earth, one with limits on taxes and limits on expensive social services for all. The new rich do not need that service. They are able to pay in cash with all the money rescued from the tax authorities back in those old-fashioned countries where they still believe in the value of social security for all; a value more and more difficult to realize as the money-people flee the country, or threaten to flee.

In addition comes the other loss for the old-fashioned states: the loss of a major cleavage. The cold war, with all its misery, its oppression of dissenters, its lack of respect for human rights, its waste of money on weapons and surveillance – that cold and sometimes not so cold war – gave purpose to some state actions. And it had also some beneficial consequences for the protection of the weak within some of the welfare states. A concern during the cold war against the USSR bloc was to keep the workers of the West satisfied, so that they should not adopt ideas from the East. Welfare arrangements might be seen by many as having a flair of socialism, but were, during the cold war, actively supported by essential parts of the Western establishment. With the end of the great cleavage, the globe has become one, and workers' rights and arrangements for social security are by many converted from being parts of a defence system in the cold war into being seen as unnecessary hindrances to economic development.

In this situation, a new type of state emerges. It is no longer a question of a strong state. The global market is strong and supposed to remain so.

And the state is belittled. The need is for the suitably weakened state. This formulation is inspired by Zygmunt Bauman's (1998) book on *Globalization*. He has this to say about the new role of the new states:

> For their liberty of movement and for their unconstrained freedom to pursue their ends, global finance, trade and the information industry depend on the political fragmentation – the *morcellement* of the world scene. They have all, one may say, developed vested interests in 'weak states', that is, in such states as are *weak* but nevertheless *remain states* . . . Weak, quasi-states can be easily reduced to the (useful) role of legal police precincts, securing a modicum of order required for the conduct of business, but need not be feared as effective brakes on the global companies' freedom.
>
> (pp. 67–8)

3.4 Crime control as the arena for presentation

The Norwegian Parliament has a special committee for legal affairs. It is an important committee for the discussion of crime. To come here, a chairperson told me, meant a different life compared to the life in most of the other committees. It meant being in the centre of public life. Telephones, letters, newspapers, radio and television – it was a new life with immense exposure; for a politician it meant to come out from the valley of shadows and into the bright sunshine.

So also is the situation in Sweden and Denmark. Crime has come to the centre of political attention. Has come, for it was not always like this. In the period after World War II, 'crime policy', or *kriminalpolitikk* as it is called in Scandinavia, was a completely misplaced term for what happened. It was not politics, or politicians, that ruled. The decisions were made by 'experts', and then, obediently, put in effect by politicians. Legal scholars had a tremendous influence. Ministers for legal affairs in Norway were until 1973 always legally educated. How could they handle legal problems, and even more, how could they have opinions on punishment, if they were not lawyers? The parliamentarians, particularly the leaders of the committee for legal affairs, also leaned heavily on the lawyers. We had one and the same person acting as chairman in the Norwegian Parliament for 20 years. He did not belong to the ruling party. The reasons he survived for so long were twofold: First, activities in the law committee were at that time not seen as a central part of politics; they were seen as technical jobs, based on expert knowledge. At that time, it was no sunshine-job to be the chairman of that committee. There was no great competition for such a position. In addition, the old chair-man was gradually seen as belonging to the legal establishment himself. Little by little, he talked as a lawyer and thought as a lawyer. He achieved fame among lawyers for being so close to them that his lack of legal education did not matter. He kept crime out of politics and politics out of crime.

But all that was before and not now.

Today, in the suitably weakened state, it is a dream of most politicians to be involved with law, particularly penal law. The explanation is close to obvious: There are so few other arenas left, arenas for the national exposure of the politicians as political figures, and for the party line. Where the dominant goal of life is money and the dominating idea is that an unregulated market economy is the road to this goal, in such a system crime becomes the major arena for what remains of politics. Here it is possible to present oneself as a person deserving votes, with values common to a population of affluent consumers.

Nearly everywhere we find fierce competition to prove oneself and one's party to be the leading one in the war against crime in general. Bill Clinton demonstrated this in his postures against crime. Tony Blair does the same. George W. Bush demonstrates it – we will soon turn to the topic of terrorism. It is generally a policy where individuals and parties attempt to overbid each other in advocating stern measures. There are so few other arenas left for exposure. What is defined as crime and its control become of overwhelming importance. The janitors of the suitably weakened states prove their worth. Crime, or rather the fight against crime, becomes indispensable in creating legitimacy in, and for, the suit-ably weakened state.

One might have thought that this ought to have been different in Scandinavia, with our tradition for thinking about welfare and the defence of the weak (Mathiesen 1985). And that it *is* different, is reflected in the low prison figures. Compared to what happens in most highly industrialized countries, our politicians show a considerable amount of moderation. The same is the case within both prosecution and courts. It is not easy to combine welfare and punishment in small countries, where it is difficult not to see each other as fellow human beings. But it is possible, if delivery of pain is seen as an instrument for the protection of the weak and vulnerable. That is what happens in the field of drugs, where the Nordic countries have not only grudgingly been forced to take part, but have been in the forefront of the war. Most visibly is this in Sweden.

3.5 Punishment in the service of welfare

At the global arena, Sweden seems to be the very incarnation of welfare. A land for generations spared from war and huge accidents. A land where the political hegemony for so long belonged to the social democrats. A land where people care for each other.

Henrik Tham (1995/2001) has described the Swedish development in this once so solidly founded welfare state. He characterizes the social democrats' attitude to penal questions as – initially – one of non-interest. The social democrats were interested in social reforms, particularly in improving the conditions of the poor. These reforms were the key to the establishment of the good society. Slowly the social democrats become more interested in penal policy, but then in reforms, particularly in the reduction of the size of the penal system. Lennart Geijer, a Swedish Minister of Justice in the 1970s, established the political goal of no more than 500 prisoners for the whole of Sweden and not 4,000 as they had at that time.

But then the tide turned. The war against drugs reached Sweden. Demands rose for severe punishments as weapons in this war. The Prime Minister at the time – Olof Palme – tried to fend off the punitive demands by pointing to the need for reform of the general conditions leading to abuse. But the penal activists had other arguments. From the far left came references to the view Karl Marx had on the *Lumpenproletariat* as the enemy of the working class. Others, also from the left – often working within the treatment institutions for drug users – pointed to Labour's established tradition for solidarity with the weak. In line with this: Youth were in need of protection, they were in danger of their lives, penal measures must prevent such a development. A drug-free society became the official goal. Step by step, the penal measures were sharpened, and not only against drugs. As Henrik Tham points out, the last 20 years has seen a complete turnabout, from demands for reduced use of imprisonment to demands for war equipment, which inevitably leads to a greater use of prisons.

In this very period, the liberals and the conservatives also entered the penal arena with demands for increased punishment. It was not obvious that this would happen. The liberals in particular have a heritage of concern for the individual human being, and for human rights. Henrik Tham suggests that this tradition might be weaker in Sweden than in other European countries, since the medieval aristocratic domain survived longer in Sweden than in most European countries. Sweden went, so to say, straight from aristocratic rule into a society run by social democrats – the liberal tradition did not gain a particularly solid hold.

This might be right. Sweden, and to some extent Norway, are exceptionally active in the war against drugs. They are so out of a social democratic tradition. There is no reason to doubt that much of the severity of penal measures against drugs is rooted in ideas about welfare and the need for protection of the weak. But the end result might be that they hurt a considerable number of those they want to protect. In a recent report, edited by Tham (2003), seven researchers are in agreement: The war against drugs in Sweden has fatal costs. One of the authors, Markus Heilig, writes (p. 41, my translation):

> It is a general belief in Sweden that we represent a progressive country when it comes to drug policy and treatment. The realities from the streets are different. And for me, as researcher, medical doctor and human being, this policy is completely unbearable.

There are well documented and efficient treatment methods available, says Heilig, but they are, for ideological reasons, not available to the majority of patients dependent on heroin. Lenke and Olsson document in the same publication death figures beyond all decency in a welfare nation, and Tham and Träskman show how the use of punishment against drugs is in complete disharmony with the usual standards.[3]

In the war against drugs, an interesting major alliance has been established. It is between Sweden and the US. Sweden provides the welfare alibi: When Sweden is so eagerly engaged in this war and is against most proposals for restrictions on the tools used in this war, then the war must be OK. It must be a war for welfare. Sweden gives legitimization, and the US gives power. Power abroad by fighting on foreign territories, as in Colombia and also Afghanistan where the opium production now is back to old levels, or through economic pressure against states seen as not sufficiently eager in the war against drugs. And of course power at home, as illustrated through the enormity of the US prison population. Jointly, the two countries contribute exceptionally large sums of money to the drug policy carried out through the United Nations,[4] and gain thereby an extraordinary influence on how this war is fought.

The war against drugs occurs in the service of high values. With such a purpose one actually also goes a long way in the control of those sections of any society usually selected for imprisonment. It is reflected in the prison population. Close to half of the prison population of Norway and Sweden is imprisoned in relation to the use or sale of drugs. By and large, they have the same characteristics as those we also earlier had in our prison systems. They are similar to the traditional lower-lower class always found in our prisons. Now they have connection with drugs as one more attribute.

3.6 A most useful Mafia

A kind and peaceful enemy is not a good enemy. Evil and dangerous is what the enemy ought to be. And strong. Sufficiently strong to give honour and homage to the hero home from war. But not so strong that the hero is not returning. The pictures of the enemy are important elements in the preparation for war. Concepts with high use-value in our connection are such as 'Mafia' and 'Organized crime'. Their exceptional lack of precision makes them useful as slogans for most types of evil forces. They are useful words in a war fought by a suitably weakened state.

*   *   *

It is just a few hours by train between Helsinki in Finland and St Petersburg in Russia. Polite Finnish customs officers, polite Russian ones. The first major stop on the Russian side is Viborg, with a railway station built like a palace. Rightly so; here the Tsar might have stopped on his tours back and forth to his Finnish province. Seconds before the train stops in St Petersburg, we pass Kresty. It means the cross, and so it functions. It is the local prison for St Petersburg, famous since the days of Anna Achmatova (1889–1966). She wrote a poem about this prison and those who were in there, among them her son. The prison is also today one of the worst in Europe, built for 2–3,000 prisoners, now with some 9,000 packed in.

*   *   *

St Petersburg is the jewel of Russia – and a dungeon. Built to please the aristocracy and display the power of the empire, and filled with wonders of art and architecture. And soaked by crime – according to tourist brochures, according to police warnings, and according to several criminological reports. And these indicators on the negative side seem to climb all the time. Killing, grave bodily harm, theft – all are on the increase all over Russia, but particularly in Moscow and St Petersburg. Behind it all stands the Mafia, or when that fails, organized crime. Whenever one goes into Russia, these concepts are introduced. Then all is said, and nothing.

So far so bad.

But it is also possible to have another view. An important researcher in this field in Scandinavia is Johan Bäckman. In several articles, recently gathered in the book *The Inflation of Crime in Russia* (Bäckman 1998a), he describes the usefulness of the image of the Mafia. Useful inside Russia, but also outside. In a chapter he calls 'The Russia-Genre as a Construction of Reality' he points to the use of the Mafia theme in Western literature, and particularly in films:

> The Russia-Genre is an extremely profitable industry. For example, *Golden Eye* 1995 has produced a world-wide profit of 350 million US dollars on a budget of 60 million US dollars. The estimated profit of Russia-Genre films in the 1990s is at least one billion US dollars in the US alone, while world-wide it is two or three billion. The profits have doubled since the 1980s.
>
> The estimate, compiled from the Internet Movie Database 1997, does not cover all the media of the Russia-Genre, such as popular literature and journalism.
>
> One might well ask whether telling stories about organized crime in Russia is in fact more profitable than the Mafia activity itself.

The image of the Russian Mafia sells well among the general public in the West. But it is also politically useful in the West. The Mafia image is much used by politicians. There are hearings in the US Congress on the theme. The old enemy picture from the cold war is gone; up comes the Russian Mafia – cool, strong, unpredictable, and therefore particularly dangerous. If the Mafia run Russia, the country is not to be trusted. Patricia Rawlinson, a British criminologist fond of Russian culture and a sharp observer of Russian realities, says (1998, p. 346):

> Although generally discredited by criminologists from the 1970s, this populist notion of 'mafia' has been given a new lease of life through the emergence and proliferation outside the former Soviet Union, of Russian organized crime. Already conversant with Cold War rhetoric and the simplistic dichotomy between capitalism and communism, the media offers an equally prejudiced and simplistic interpretation of the Russian 'mafia' and threatens to obfuscate and consequently exacerbate the actual dangers presented by its proliferation.

Rawlinson also describes (pp. 354–5) how the media struggle to present a dramatized picture of 'mafia-types':

> Demands for interviews with Russian gangsters far outweigh the supply and have consequently spawned a new industry for the ever-watchful entrepreneur. Low-ranking gang members and even 'straight' guys play 'hood' for journalists in return for high interview fees.

But, as said, also inside Russia continuous attention is given to the idea of the Mafia. Bäckman suggests several explanations. One is that life is not easy in Russia; conditions have not changed with the promised speed. The Mafia is a handy explanation. In addition comes the phenomenon Bäckman calls 'The Inflated Mafia'. The country has lived for 70 years with an ideology claiming that striving for private profit was equal to crime. Suddenly, that same activity is elevated to model behaviour in the approaching capitalist Russia. No wonder that some ambivalence surfaces, and that some of those succeeding are given other names. In addition comes a Russian tradition of personalized relationships, says Bäckman. When in need of help, one goes to friends, or friends of friends. So also in business, and in relations with authorities. It can be seen as a close-knit system of privileged relationships and is given the name of Mafia behaviour. But it can also be seen as a system based on trust, not only on contract. With a totalitarian past and now in a weakened state, personalized relations are a rational adaptation to insecurity. But at the same time this opens for unfair privileges, and an easily understood anger by those outside the networks of trust. Again Mafia is an easily applied term.

The Mafia image is also a highly useful tool for Russian authorities by giving power back to the Ministry of the Interior and in particular to the various branches of the police. Russia was until recently a policeman's paradise. The police knew where everybody lived. And where people lived, they stayed. Ordinary people were not allowed to move. Farmers lived under bondage until 1861, but in reality all Russians did so from 1932 and until quite recently. As Shelley (1980) explained in an earlier article, while the system still operated:

> Passport regulations and population policies govern the lives of all Soviet citizens . . . The internal passport controls mobility as well as residence; it is required to purchase plane tickets, long distance train tickets, and a room in a hotel. Individuals without passports are restricted exclusively to local travel.

> (p. 113)

With ideas of a Mafia, it is easier to preserve these forms of control.

3.7 Words as weapons

Do I claim there are no Mafia?

No. I limit my claim to an agreement with Gilinsky (1997) that Mafia is an extremely badly defined concept. And it is just because of this looseness that the Mafia concept is so useful outside Russia, for the film industry as well as for foreign departments, but also inside Russia for frustrated citizens as well as for the Ministry of Internal Affairs.

But tools useful for so many purposes are for that very reason unable to help us to answer questions such as: Is there much Mafia behaviour in Russia? Does it increase? What will the future be? Mafia is a conceptual weapon. We can understand more of social life by observing how the concept is used. But, just as with the concept of crime, the Mafia concept does not help us to understand the prevalence of, and conditions for, unwanted behaviour in a society.

It cannot be doubted that in Russia as in other countries, deplorable acts, terrible acts, or acts clearly in conflict with national or international law are often carried out by more than one person. Sometimes they are carried out by many, sometimes by people of the same age, sex, nationality or ethnic origin, sometimes organized in hierarchies, sometimes with internal control, sometimes claiming monopoly over a territory, sometimes paying authorities not to intervene, sometimes killing opponents or victims. But with all these variations, we are confronted with severe problems of classification. What in this list qualifies for the labels 'Mafia' or 'organized crime'?

- What are the organizational features that qualify: size, hierarchy, internal control, type of territory – national or international . . .
- Some of these organizations will behave deplorably in all their activities, some most of the time, some in a minority of occasions, some hardly ever. Again: What sort of activity level qualifies an organization to be called a Mafia organization or one of organized crime?
- Some organizations show a decline in illegal activities over time. At what point does such an organization convert from being a Mafia organization into being an ordinary business?

Hawkins (1969) has compared organized crime and God. The two have one common feature: Their existence cannot be disproved. I would like to add: They also have in common that they can be used or misused for a large range of purposes.

* * *

As a well-defined phenomenon, which can be clearly described, measured, compared to other phenomena, the Mafia does not exist. But I have met its members. Or some close to them. They look dangerous. *And so they wish.*

3.8 The Mafia as a cultural product

I met some of them recently on a narrow road close to the Baltic Sea. Their elegant car had made a stop. Our old bus could not pass. They performed a ballet with studied provocative slowness to get back into the car, mastering the difficult task of closing the doors of the car and thus making passing possible. Another ballet is performed close to plush restaurants: A streamlined Porsche appears with some other cars. Of course, all being double-parked. Some huge men come out of them, elegantly dressed, but nothing compared to the accompanying long-legged ladies, their silk and furs and gold combined with a body language conveying an aura of arrogance and provocation.

For a long time I thought of bad manners, eventually of the nouveau riche. But then I came to think of Joan Neuberger.

Joan Neuberger (1993) has written a beautiful book on *Hooliganism: Crime, Culture and Power in St Petersburg 1900–1914*. Hooliganism is a word imported into Russia at the end of the eighteenth century and put into use without any major change. The author opens her book with a quote from a newspaper in 1913:

> A terrible situation has seized our city and, under the name of hooliganism, takes forms that threaten the security of our society. Malicious assaults, fist fights, knifings, disgusting forms of depravity, and inexcusable drunkenness occur on our streets – and are committed not only by grown men but by women and children as well.

And, says Joan Neuberger in her own opening remarks:

> In published discussions disparate crimes were lumped together because they seemed to reveal a new mentality of defiance among petty criminals and later among the lower classes generally. On the streets the hooligans themselves were forging a new kind of power . . . by exploiting their ability to mock and intimidate the respectable pedestrians who stood above them on the social and economic ladder. Hooligans did not defy institutions of power directly but used public and symbolic behaviour to challenge existing hierarchies of everyday life. They threatened established forms of social authority openly, but they also reached below the surface to tap some of the as yet unarticulated hostilities, fears and insecurities emerging in the new Russian metropolis.

(p. 2)

As with the concept of hooliganism, the Mafia is also a concept from the West put into immediate use in its Western form. A new concept, a new role. Maybe some of the behaviour was there first, in embryonic form. Then came the concept. Then more people began to fit the description. Slowly it became a role with a developed manuscript for behaviour.

Inspired by Neuberger, we might try to advance a bit further. Read as a message, we must find out what the nouveau riche attempt to say with their demeanour. Hooliganism was protest. One that police, criminologists and social workers eagerly tried to eradicate. These new and very rich glittering young people might be seen as a functional equivalent to the more advanced among the graffiti painters in the West. Their art – the Western graffiti – can be seen as a negation of the dominant culture, aesthetically as well as morally. Signs and symbols represent powerful aspects of our reality. Graffiti on the walls of the city hall, or on the door of the cathedral, can be seen as a counter-attack, an attempt to create an alternative understanding of the world (Skardhamar 1998) (Høigård 2002). Russia has lived under an official ideology of the Puritan work ethic for 70 years. The Stachanow worker was the ideal. This ideal is deeply ingrained in the soul of so many. Now we smash it, and drive our Porsche wherever we want.

But then again by doing this, they strengthen the ideals they smear, and they strengthen the state.

* * *

I have, helped by Bäckman, pointed to the usefulness of the concept of Mafia. It 'explains' anomalies and it gives increased power to the state. But the concept and its assumed realities also have their costs.

In particular, all the muddled Mafia talk creates a general impression that the frequency of unwanted acts such as killing and theft is particularly high in Russia. Simply, that there is more unwanted behaviour of this type in Russia than in the West.

But is that not the case?

It is difficult to interpret the available information. My general impression, but it is not more than an impression, is that the level of interpersonal violence is high in Russia compared to Western Europe, but not compared to the USA and Latin America. But the content of Russian violence is also very similar to what is found in Western Europe. It is mostly violence within the family, or inside or outside bars. And it is violence dripping with alcohol. It is rooted in miserable life conditions, combined with a cultural tradition of heavy drinking. Kauko Aromaa and Andri Ahven (1995) find the same in Estonia. Most killings are family killings, not Mafia killings.

Acts given the meaning of being thefts and robberies might also be on the increase. Tourists represent here a particularly attractive target with their visible wealth. Slowly, Russia is becoming an ordinary class-divided country with the troubles of that type of society. But based both on personal observations and on extensive discussions with Russians and Scandinavian friends and colleagues visiting the country, I am far from convinced that the situation in Russian towns differs vastly from what we find in the West. A further confirmation of this is found in the study by Aromaa and Lehti (1995).

Some might find these observations in severe conflict with the media picture. Am I too kind to a neighbouring country? Do I hide the problems? What is said here does not fit in with the media reports. They are probably dangerous, those Russians?

They are at least not so when they go to Finland. One million of them do so each year. Bäckman (1998b) conveyed some news on the result of this invasion at the annual Nordic research seminar in 1998:

> In spite of the annual volume of one million visitors from Russia,[5] the statistics on crime and conviction show that annually only about one percent of suspects and convicts are citizens of Russia. The majority of the crimes committed by Russians are traffic offences and petty larcenies . . . in 1996 only three Russians and four Swedes were suspected of murder in Finland, while the number of Finnish suspects was over 500 . . . Out of 3,200 prisoners, only six are citizens of Russia.

The dramatic increase in the number of Russian motorists traversing the roads of Finland[6] has not resulted in the expected massacres: in 1997 over 400 individuals died in the Finnish traffic, but only nine deaths were attributable to Russian drivers.

3.9 A block against understanding

The problematic nature of the Mafia concept was again revealed in the early months of 2003. This time in Beograd in the former Yugoslavia. Prime Minister Zoran Djindjic was shot – by the Mafia, we were told. A war against Mafia crime was called for.

Forgotten was the history of recent developments in Yugoslavia. An international blockade of the country had for a long period been met with a vast amount of smuggling across the borders. That activity was a state-approved activity which had made life in Yugoslavia possible. Smugglers made profit, but were also seen as a complete necessity in the political situation. This does not mean that those people were seen only as heroes or behaved with dignity. An underground economy, as here developed, is one where the official bodies of the state cannot be used to handle internal conflicts. Internal conflicts will erupt, violence will blossom. The situation becomes particularly complicated if external circumstances change; some sort of peace might emerge, as in Northern Ireland, or the blockade comes to an end, as in Yugoslavia. The state re-appears and attempts to control the earlier important, but now illegal, activities. Also to Prime Minister Zoran Djindjic the smugglers were important, once. But then came the need to bring them back into ordin-ary society.

Here several courses of action are possible: One is to accept that these groupings at one point in time had been important for the survival of the country, give them some honour for past accomplishments, and amnesties for their misdeeds. This might, but with obvious possibilities for failing, slowly bring them and their talents back into ordinary society. But they might, with good reason, be hated by many. Often they are also connected to certain political groupings. Close at hand here, comes the Mafia concept, and if that sticks, to stage a war against them. The Mafia is a more respectable target than political opponents. The choice of con-cepts influences the understanding of a phenomenon, and thereby also how to meet it.

3.10 Terror

The 'Mafia' concept is not the only one useful for state purposes. The 'Terrorist' concept is another, well illustrated in the war in Chechnya. The enemies were not soldiers, and of course not freedom fighters or reli-gious absolutists, but simply terrorists. In the words of Sergei Kovalev (2000), President of the Institute for Human Rights in Moscow and member of the Russian State Duma:

> Russian politicians began to use a new language – the argot of the criminal world . . . Old terms took on a completely new meaning. Thus, the word 'terrorist' quickly ceased to mean someone belonging to a criminal underground group whose goal was political murder. Now the word came to mean 'an armed Chechen' anywhere. Military reports from Chechnya put it plainly: 'A group of three thousand terrorists has been surrounded in Gudermes'; 'two and a half thousand terrorists were liquidated in Shali'. And the war itself came to be called nothing less than the 'antiterrorist special operation of the Russian troops'.

The whole situation has led to extreme police surveillance of all persons suspected of Chechen descent in Moscow. It has also helped Vladimir Putin to the top of Russian policy, and will, according to Kovalev, probably lead Russia into an authoritarian police regime that will preserve the formal characteristics of democracy, but at the same time lead to reforms towards a market economy.

*   *   *

I wrote this before 11 September 2001. And after that date, it was simply a matter of continuing the line of argument.

3.11 Trolls

So much changed on 11 September. Not because of our knowledge of the three hijacked aeroplanes or of our imagination of what must have occurred inside those planes during the last minutes of their flight. Not because of the two towers in New York that collapsed. Not because of the 4,000 human beings annihilated. Atrocities, yes. But nothing special, compared to the inhuman history of humans. Nothing compared to World Wars I and II. Nothing compared to Auschwitz, Hiroshima and Nagasaki, Dresden, the Gulags, Vietnam, Cambodia. Nothing.

Why then?

Because it did not only hit New York or the USA. It hit us, the West. It came out of the sky, beautifully shining in the sun. So elegant. Maybe it was the contrast between form and content. It ought to have come out of the dark misty underground. The earth ought to have opened and out should have come a bony arm of vengeance, an arm and a hand from those that have not taken part in our big meal, the years of material progress in the Western world. Revenge, and a new balance. That would have been easier to understand.

President Bush has another explanation than the one of the bony arm up from the ground. I quote from his much celebrated Address to a Joint Session of Congress and the American People on 20 September 2001:

> Americans are asking, why do they hate us? They hate what we see right here in this chamber – a democratically elected government. Their leaders are self-appointed. They hate our freedoms – our freedom of religion, our freedom of speech, our freedom to vote and assemble and disagree with each other.

Hand in hand with this interpretation of the occurrences, comes a dark terminology. On 5 December, the President states:

The evil ones still intend to harm America . . . Now it is a time for the free world to stand up and defend the freedoms that these evil ones hate.

With these words from the President, we are back to familiar ground in criminology: evil people, maybe monsters. We have to drive them out. Or exterminate them. Or again, as expressed by Bush on 20 September:

the only way to defeat terrorism as a threat to our way of life is to stop it, eliminate it, and destroy it where it grows (Applause).

This terminology has, however, some problems attached. Evil people *are their own explanation*. The discussion comes to a stop, the phenomenon is understood, there is no further need for intellectual efforts.

Also, with evil people, the next step becomes close to obvious. They have to be eliminated. War is the natural answer. War and extermination.

* * *

In the Nordic countries we have our own breed of monsters, not quite as bad as terrorists, not evil all the way, but close to it. Most often they are a bit dumb. We call them Trolls. You do not treat Trolls. Nor do you train them, or put them into programmes for rehabilitation. To be a Troll is a condition.

The central actors of 11 September were not called Trolls. They were called 'terrorists', with Osama bin Laden as the 'super-terrorist'. This is an old theme in criminology. They are seen as terrorists. But are people their acts, and eventually, what parts of their acts? Is stealing the major characteristic of a thief – or killing the major characteristic of one that has killed? Some people come close to being their acts. Gandhi and Jesus are supposed to have been of that type. But most often we are able to see that most people are multidimensional. A person might have committed some acts we deplore, but he also has other sides. When one is open to this, it is not quite so easy to see the other person as a monster, even if we think some aspects of his or her behaviour might be particularly unacceptable.

But this claim for differentiation between act and person is often controversial, inside criminology as well. We have our own monsters. In criminology, they are called psychopaths. Of all psychopaths, the one with the greatest proximity to a monster is, in my language, called *følelseskald psykopat*. I suppose the English words for it would be 'a psychopath without feelings'. I have never met such a person, but some psychiatrists seem to meet them again and again.

* * *

Orham Panuk has an alternative explanation to those of President Bush. Panuk (2001) is a novelist from Istanbul. In the 15 November issue of the *New York Review of Books*, he writes:

> It is neither Islam nor even poverty itself that directly engenders support for terrorists whose ferocity and ingenuity are unprecedented in human history; it is, rather, the crushing humiliation that has infected the third-world countries.
>
> At no time in history has the gulf between rich and poor been so wide . . . [and] . . . at no time in history have the lives of the rich been so forcefully brought to the attention of the poor through television and Hollywood films.

*   *   *

The Norwegian Trolls have one peculiar point of vulnerability. They are endangered by sunshine. At the first glimmer of sunlight that might find them, they crack or turn to stone. That is the explanation of the many strange stone formations you find if you walk in the Norwegian mountains.

The pictures of monsters are difficult to preserve if you come to know them. Ordinary acquaintance might do, or a scientific one. When we understand somewhat more of people's behaviour, particularly when, or if, we are able to see ourselves in the other person's behaviour, then the monster dissolves.

But for state actions they might seem well suited.

4 Incarceration as an answer

4.1 Social arrangements for the promotion of crime

If my power was that of a dictator and if I had the urge to construct a situation for the promotion of crime, then I would have shaped our societies in a form very close to what we find in a great number of modern states.

We have constructed societies where it is particularly easy, and also in the interest of many, to define unwanted behaviour as acts of crime – this in contrast to being examples of bad, mad, eccentric, exceptional, inde-cent or just unwanted acts. We have also shaped these societies in ways that encourage unwanted forms of behaviour, and at the same time reduce possibilities for informal control. This whole situation is obviously one that will influence the prison situation in the industrialized world. It will first and foremost create a situation with increased pressure on the prison systems within most of these societies. But this is not without exceptions. The size of the prison population in any society is also a result of past national history, of major political ideas, and not at least the willingness to look for solutions other than the penal ones.

Table 4.1 presents the number of prisoners per 100,000 inhabitants in some major areas of our globe. The countries within each area are ranked according to size of their prison populations, in each case with the high-raters at the top. Most of the figures are taken from the useful statistics gathered by Roy Walmsley (2003 and continuously updated and made available through the International Centre for Prison Studies).[1] Some figures are based on material I have obtained in direct contact with representatives from various prison administrations in countries I have visited. Some of my figures differ from those made available from Roy Walmsley and the International Centre for Prison Studies, but these differences are not of importance for the reasoning in what follows. Most figures are from the years 2000–2002.

* * *

Table 4.1 Prison population rate per 100,000 of national populations

Western Europe

England and Wales	139
Portugal	135
Spain	126
Italy	100
France	99
Netherlands	93
Germany	91
Ireland	86
Austria	85
Belgium	85
Greece	80
Switzerland	69
Denmark	66
Sweden	64
Norway	62
Finland	60
Iceland	37

Central and Eastern Europe

Russian Federation	607
Belarus	554
Ukraine	406
Latvia	361
Estonia	328
Lithuania	327
Moldova	300
Poland	260
Romania	215
Georgia	196
Hungary	176
Czech Republic	159
Slovakia	139
Bulgaria	114
Turkey	89
Slovenia	56

North America

USA	730
Canada	116

Central America

Cuba	500 (estimate)
Belize	459
Panama	359
Costa Rica	229
Honduras	172
El Salvador	158
Mexico	156
Nicaragua	143
Guatemala	71

South America

Chile	204
Uruguay	166
Argentina	154
Brazil	137
Colombia	126
Peru	104
Bolivia	102
Paraguay	75
Venezuela	62
Ecuador	59

Oceania

New Zealand	155
Australia	112

The huge variation between countries is one of the most striking features in the table. We find Iceland at the very bottom and the USA and Russia as the absolute champions in incarceration among industrialized countries.

We will come back to this major table several times in what follows, but let us here, as a first question, ask if they have something in common, the two giant incarcerators.

4.2 The great incarcerators

The USA has today more than 2.1 million prisoners. This means 730 prisoners per 100,000 inhabitants – more than 0.7 per cent. The increase has been unbelievable since 1975. The growth has slowed down recently, but has not come to a full stop. In addition to those imprisoned come 4.7 million on bail, probation and parole. This means that 6.8 million of the US population in 2003 is under some sort of control of the institution for penal law. Of the total population in the US, 2.4 per cent is at any time under the control of this institution. Among those 15 years or older, 3.1 per cent of the population is under this sort of control.

Russia is solidly behind, and increasingly so. On 1 January 2003, they had 866,000 prisoners or 607 per 100,000 inhabitants. Two years earlier, they had more than a million prisoners, or 680 per 100,000 inhabitants. The number of prisoners waiting for trial went from 282,000 in year 2000 to 145,000 in 2003.[2] It is the prisons for people waiting for trial that are the particular chambers of horror in Russia. Vivian Stern (1999) has edited a book on Russian prison conditions. 'Sentenced to die' is the title. This formulation captures the essence. Sleeping in three shifts in damp rooms with hundreds of prisoners does not give the best of protection against an explosion of TB, HIV and AIDS within these establishments, an explosion that later will affect the whole Russian population. After sentencing, those sentenced are moved out of Moscow to the colonies, the former Gulags. Here conditions are considerably better.

The Duma, the Russian parliament, passed several important laws in May 2001 with the intention to reduce the prison population by a third. The effects of these new laws are easy to observe. Prior to these reforms, the average space in the remand prisons was less than 1 square metre per person. Today the average is 3.5 square metres, while the norm laid down by the public health authorities is 4 square metres (Kalinin 2002, p. 17).

4.3 Common features

What do they have in common these two states, in addition to being high on incarceration?

A first and obvious similarity between the USA and Russia is simply their size, in land, power and population. With all this, there is also created a foundation for organizational patterns that encourage *social* distance. At the broad avenues of Moscow there is a special lane in the middle, reserved for the President and the cortège of dignitaries following him. At the small scale of a visiting scholar and on ordinary bumpy roads in Russia, I have mentally been in the same social setting. For several hours, we had one police car with sirens and blue lights in front and one behind. Ordinary cars were forced to stop; here we come, the emperors – or at least someone somehow related to those high up.

But not only in Moscow. Western capitals have their helicopters for their rulers as alternatives to the reserved middle lane. And they have their quota of close-knit associations for power-holders. I have vivid memories from an occasion in Washington DC. It was a setting filled with particularly dignified persons. My lasting memory from the evening was the welcome speech by the host. Many were invited and most came, but some had been unable to attend. But they had all – and we got the name for every invited dignitary not there – they had all personally phoned the host and explained why they were not able to attend. No secretary could do. I felt as in a party for those close to the King. You were supposed to be there, or personally give overwhelmingly good reasons for absence. Otherwise you might be at the edge of expulsion.

All this is in a way obvious: In large social systems, and I am talking about pyramidal ones, a relatively small part of the population will be at the very top. Or, it demands at least exceptional political ingenuity to create conditions for a broader representation. With a small group at the top, those up there will become extremely important to each other. But then, at the same time, the logic of the situation is that they become distant from those they rule. Social distance is one of the conditions for heavy use of the penal system.

* * *

Another similarity between Russia and the US: They have in common a weak position of their judges. In the US, this is obviously the case. Compared to judges in Western Europe, those in the US have gradually lost their power to the politicians and to the prosecutors. The US system of sentencing tables gives the politicians – who are those deciding on the sentencing tables – detailed regulatory power in deciding on punishment.[3] So does also the extensive use of mandatory sentencing laws. If the facts of the case are clear, the judge has nearly no room for discretion. In a survey of United States judges, 86 per cent of district judges and chief probation officers agreed that the guidelines give too much discretion and control to prosecutors. Some 71.5 per cent were moderately or strongly opposed to retaining the current system of mandatory sentencing guidelines.[4]

Judges in the US are also to a large extent directly elected. But the political process is based on limited participation in the election process. More than 4 million people, including 1.4 million black men, cannot vote because they have a criminal record. Many will never regain their right to vote (Mauer and Chesney-Lind 2002). For a politician, here is not much to gain. In contrast to the judge, the prosecutor has kept his power. He can make a deal with the suspect, drop parts of the charge if the suspect admits certain other acts. In a system with sentencing tables, the prosecutor can heavily influence the end result.

But also in the classical Eastern European situation, the judge will to a large extent be dependent on political powers to get the job, and retain it. Of particular importance here is the prosecutor. This is one of the major reasons for the great number of people in detention waiting for trial. Russian and Belarus judges hesitate to acquit. Instead, they return cases to the prosecutor. While the prosecutor thinks, the prisoner is waiting it out. Often it takes years.

I cannot prove my point on the balance of power. But I observe, and I listen. I experienced an exposure of this situation during a meeting in Belarus in May 2002. Belarus will soon become the leading country of incarceration in Europe if Russia reduces as planned. A few years ago, Belarus had 500 prisoners per 100,000 inhabitants. In 2001 they had 560. In absolute figures this means 56,000 prisoners. Belarus has 10 million inhabitants.

In this meeting in Belarus, the prison administration attended, together with several directors of prisons and colonies. So did also some judges and prosecutors. Towards the end of the meeting, a little woman far down the table asked for the floor. She had been a judge, but quit, and told us why. While she was speaking, the atmosphere in the room became ice-cold, but she continued. She was trained in law, and had learnt her lesson: The major goal was to catch a maximum number of criminals and then jail them. So she did, as a police jurist. She did it so well that she advanced. She became a judge, with the proper status and apartment belonging to this kind of job. Again she knew the rules of the game: To get the accused sentenced. Lenient punishments and an acquittal rate of more than a tiny percentage would be unacceptable. At one point in time, she saw her dependence on the state she was supposed to control, and quit.

*   *   *

A further common feature between some of the leading incarcerators is the root their prison systems have in *servitude* or *slavery*.

Liberty for Some is the title Scott Christianson (1998) has given his important book on this theme. In the simplification necessary here and now, it is not much of an exaggeration to say that when the blacks in the south were set free, also to move, they took their seats in the front of the bus and went north, to the inner cities, and from there to the prisons. Per 100,000 black males, 3,535 were in prison at year-end 2001, against 462 per 100,000 of white males.[5] Large prison figures are linked to the tradition of slavery.

The very same phenomena can also be seen in Russian history, a history that here includes Belarus. There were not extremely many prisoners during the era of the Tsar. They had an alternative. They had servitude. Peasants were the property of their masters. They could not move or marry without the consent of the aristocrat who owned them. This meant that the lower classes were under severe control. And should this control fail, or non-peasants misbehave, they had Siberia. The colonization of that huge country was to a large extent done by prisoners.[6] In this perspective, the Gulags were not that much of a break with the past. They were not first and foremost for dissenters. They were production units, filled with males from the lower classes. The servitude found its new form.

So, basically, these are similar systems for the maxi/maxi-incarcerators. And they are developing similar social and cultural traits: their particular music, language, clothes. There exists a FM radio station in Moscow where most of the talk and music is prison talk and prison music. The same is obviously the case in parts of the US culture. There seem also to be similarities in the inner organization of these systems. At least for the Russian system, it seems clear that it everywhere, except earlier among most of the political dissidents, develops extremely stratified systems with the untouchable losers at the very bottom. Due to better material conditions, more possibilities for isolation of individual prisoners and also more guards per inmate, this might be different in most US systems, even though the many reports on gang wars indicate that authorities are far from having complete control.

* * *

But there are also differences. Most importantly, the use-value of prisons differs among the high incarcerators.

Russia is, and has for some time, been in trouble with its prisons and colonies. The colonies are simply not profitable any more. We might dislike it, but the Gulags were essential for the Russian war efforts in 1940–5. They were also possible to operate with some sort of efficiency in command economy functioning in the USSR after World War II (or the great Patriotic War as it is called in the East). But in a market economy, they cannot compete. In the Russia of today, the prison system therefore represents a great drain on the economy.

Laura Piacentini (2002) has worked to find out what happened to the Russian colonies when the economic system changed. She conveyed two interesting observations. First, adaptation to the new situation was dependent on distance from Moscow. The further away, the freer was the situation of the local prison administration; inspectors from Moscow were few and far between. Close to Moscow, the situation was different. Here, they had to play to the tunes of the central administrators. These were tunes well known in penology. The colonies had no more work to offer, large factory halls were literally empty, or with small groups of prisoners fiddling with some minor tasks in a corner of the premises. The answer from all penological theory, as well as from the central prison administration, was clear and powerful: Prisoners are here to be changed into law-abiding citizens. Therefore, the colony must offer treatment and education. But in Russian colonies, as in most penal establishments around the world, this turned out to be mere words.

Quite different was the situation in inner Siberia, far from the watching eyes of the central administration. The situation had been difficult to the extreme in the years after 1990. In the colonies, as in ordinary places for work, it had passed months without payment for the staff. Parallel to this, it had also been a critical lack of food, clothes and heating for the prisoners. In this situation, an elaborate system of barter was created. Local colonies scrutinized the local communities for tasks to be done; they had hungry prisoners willing to do nearly everything for a return in something the colony could use for survival.

Gradually, this developed some of the colonies in the periphery of Russia into rather efficient units for production. And here comes the dilemma for those who feel competent on penal matters: These colonies do not offer treatment. Bad, according to theory and international conventions. But they offer work, even food. But then to the other side of the coin, and it is here we come close to a new similarity between the USA and Russia: The danger in this situation is that here, solidly planted in both the giant incarcerators, is laid the foundation for a new system of forced labour.

In contrast to the Russian situation, the US can more easily afford its great prison population. To many in the US, the building and running of prisons means profit. This is a major point in my book *Crime Control as Industry* (Christie 2000). Recently, it has also been described cases where prisons inside the USA prove they can compete with Third World countries in offering cheap labour to the US industry in general. And it is, of course, better that prisoners eat than starve. It is also better that they work than suffer through idle hours. But it is a danger in these obvious advantages. It is convenient for authorities that they work. A captive workforce combines in a beautiful way the need for control of the lower classes with the need for inexpensive labour. It may lead states into temptations. It may lead to revivals of the institution of slavery.

4.4 On welfare

The giant incarcerators have been our point of departure for this chapter. But our Table 4.1 on prison populations does also open for other important questions and concerns. Of particular interest is what we find concerning the difference between the US and Canada. The difference here is close to unbelievable. Canada has 116 prisoners per 100,000 inhabitants, against the US with their 730. Two countries so close and still so different. Joint border from coast to coast, same language, mostly same religion, to some extent same content in the media, and also with much of the same ideals when it comes to money and style of life. How can we explain these differences in volume of incarceration? Even if the US had been *without* any overrepresentation of blacks in its prisons, it would have had more than three times the prison rate of Canada.

First, and before any attempts to explain, it is plainly important to register that the exceptional status of Canada is possible! Canada is a highly developed, well functioning, modern state. They have their troubles with crime as other modern states. They have politicians using crime problems as an agenda for self-presentation. Nonetheless, they have a volume of prisoners at one-sixth of their neighbour further south! And this difference has increased during the past years. Canada is steadily decreasing its prison population, while the US continuously is on the increase. When it comes to the volume of crime control, we are not up to destinies, but to political decisions open to choice.

And then, what is so peculiar to Canada?

It is embarrassing, but I have no clear answers, again only some hunches, this time based on a long life of visits to that country.

First, to visit Canada is for a Scandinavian very much as visiting one of the other Scandinavian countries. A bit dull, perhaps. Well regulated, orderly behaviour, polite relationships.

Second, penetrating the system a bit, one also finds another basic similarity: Canada is simply a welfare state. They have it all – old age pension, health insurance, leave of absence before birth and months thereafter, unemployment benefits. Of course, there are defects in the system, and vivid discussions on how to mend the defects eventually reduce the safety net for the poor. But the situation of the poor is fundamentally different in Canada and the US. Canada's welfare system is defended from the very top of the political establishment. Increased income inequality in the United States has not taken place in Canada, 'due to the offsetting influence of government transfers' (Sharpe 2000, p. 158).

Related to this is a third difference. Canada has for years had a staff of civil servants with a conscious policy of keeping the prison population under control. I have a personal experience here, being involved in meetings in the Ministry of Finance in Ottawa on the budget for their prison system. All ministries had been ordered to cut their budgets, but those responsible for law and order said it was impossible: They had to increase their budget since crime increased! But was it impossible – that was the question I was invited to comment on. The question led to fascinating discussions on how to reduce harm – all sorts of harm – in the Canadian society, and for what price.

As a conclusion: To use the penal system as a functional alternative to social welfare seems not to be a major alternative in the Canadian society.

4.5 East and West in Europe

If we again take a look at the table and then concentrate on the European arena, two observations are striking. First: The major difference in prison figures is between East and West. Only four countries in Western Europe have more than 100 prisoners per 100,000 of their population, while the majority of the Eastern European countries are above this level.

But then, as the second observation, we find huge differences also inside the Eastern European camp. Next to the Russian Federation and Belarus, we find at the top first the Ukraine, and then the Baltic republics, all with figures of 300 and more. At the very bottom we find Slovenia – that little country has a prison population at a level with the Nordic countries, and has had this position for years.

The general picture is clear: Russia is the super-incarcerator in Europe, then follow the former members of the Soviet Union. Visiting prisons in these countries, it is striking how similar they are in social organization and material form to the prisons in Russia. Behind these core countries, with lower relative figures of prisoners, but still high, we find those formerly independent states that up to the end of the cold war belonged to the Eastern bloc.

These countries are in so many ways squeezed in between East and West. I have, in *Crime Control as Industry* (2000), described how Finland shortly after World War II made a conscious decision to leave Eastern Europe, also when it came to penal policy. And they succeeded; they have now for years had lower prison figures than Denmark, Norway and Sweden. But, of course, Finland was during the cold war outside the Eastern bloc, their penal policy was an instrument in their struggle to link themselves to Scandinavia.

But it is clear that the same struggles around penal policy now also go on in the other countries of the former Eastern bloc. Poland is one of the interesting examples.

4.6 Polish rhythms

Seen from a criminological perspective, Figure 4.1 is a treasure – and a grim reality for those behind the figures.[7] It is a diagram of the total number of prisoners in Poland from 1945 until October 2002. Three features of the diagram are remarkable.

First, the rhythm in the line. From a start close to the bottom in 1945, it reached its first peak in 1950 with 98,000 prisoners. Six years later it was down to 35,000 then up again in 1963 to 105,000. The maximum came in

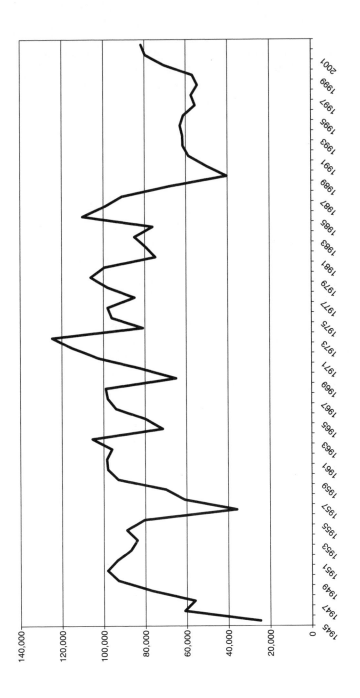

Figure 4.1 Prison population in Poland 1945–2002

1973 with 125,000 prisoners. Like this it ran until 1989, when it again was down, this time to 40,000.

In my interpretation, this is a picture of a prison system without ordinary back doors, without release procedures to use when the internal pressure on the system becomes too strong. A repressive state, strong prosecutors, stern judges – it was easier to say yes to imprisonment than to say no. But tensions build up. There were limits to the number of prisoners that could be accommodated, and also to the number that could be given meaningful work. And prisoners protested. Several riots occurred. The rhythmic answers to this were amnesties. Big ones in 1956, 1964, 1969, 1974, 1977, 1981 – and particularly in 1989, the year when the wall between East and West crumbled. Figure 4.1 illustrates how badly suited prison figures are as indicators of the crime situation in a country. Here it is bluntly clear how the prison population is a reflection of political decisions. Other countries handle this matter more discreetly.

Another fascinating development in the diagram is the period after 1989. The old regime was broken. Freedom, now also for the prisoners!

But it did not last, at the low level of 40,000 prisoners, but seemed for a period to stabilize around 55–60,000. These were the years of the political movement – later political party – with the name Solidarity, obviously also with prisoners. But then the new freedom became old, and so also the trend in the diagram. From 1999 and until October 2002 the figures have, to say it in the exact figures, gone up from 56,765 to 81,654. This is the figure I have used in Table 4.1 where we find Poland with 260 prisoners per 100,000 inhabitants. But in reality, the situation is even more extreme. Prisons are jammed. In the last months of 2002 the official estimate was that 18,000 persons were on the waiting list for serving their prison sentences. This is probably a large underestimate. Had those at the waiting list also been included, the Polish prison figures would again have passed their 100,000. Once more.

What has happened?

First: Amnesties was seen as belonging to the past, a crude instrument to correct for failures in the system. And it can, rightly, be argued that amnesties are not the best of all solutions. Great numbers of prisoners are released at the same time, putting the system for social assistance under sudden and dramatic pressure. But that strain has, of course, to be weighed against the strain of a dramatically increasing prison population.

A second explanation of the increase in prison figures is simply that Poland is being partially 'Westernized'. The old penal system is still there, the police, prosecutors, judges – no great purge took place after 1989. But in this very situation come the elements discussed in earlier chapters: Poland is on its way towards mono-culture. And a great number of politicians in Poland as elsewhere in the West use the crime arena for self-presentation. In this endeavour, they receive perfect assistance from the media. As Maria Los (2002) states, a radical shift has taken place in the mass media profile, from *good news* in state propaganda to *bad news* in private media. And she continues:

> For a population used to a criminal justice system characterized by routine detention of suspects, disregard for legal niceties, long sentences and a ban on public criticism, these developments [the exposure of the bad news] understandably produced images of a system verging on chaos or collapse.
>
> (p. 166)

My estimate, and I say this with particular reference to the diagram, is that this is a prison system in great risk of severe turmoil. Poland is now to enter the European Union. This will inevitably lead to a great reduction in the number of farmers. The surplus labour will move towards the towns. Social problems will increase. The pressure on the prisons will increase. Amnesties have regularly followed prison riots. Riot will come, and amnesties will follow. But this is a type of reform with great costs.

4.7 England and Wales – so close to Eastern Europe

We have seen that East is East, and West is West, also when it comes to prison figures. But not completely. Slovenia belongs to the Nordic countries. But surprisingly, England and Wales seem to be on a steady course towards East European standards. In 2003, England and Wales have 139 prisoners per 100,000. The figures are steadily rising, with some 600 new prisoners every week.[8] A few years back, Portugal was the leading incarcerator in Western Europe. But that was before, not now. England and Wales have entered Eastern Europe in the meaning that they have passed Bulgaria in relative number of prisoners, and now stand even to Slovakia. Nothing indicates they are about to turn. They have passed Canada, that state previously so close to them, and they have soon – in relative figures – twice as many prisoners as their close neighbour Ireland. They have since long lost connection with the historical period when Winston Churchill and his likeminded looked at imprisonment with considerable suspicion (Bennet 2003) and saw to it that their figures were kept among the lowest in Western Europe. England's similarity to the US is also visible through colours inside the prisons. One in every 100 black British adults is now in prison according to the latest Home Office figures.[9]

Attempting to understand this situation, I feel the handicaps of the combination of closeness and a large portion of love – a solid base for blindness. But of course, I cannot escape observing that step by step, England and Wales have changed important elements in their system.

First of all, they are in a process of radical adaptation to the unidimensional society. All are better off, compared to the period just after World War II, but the social differences within the population have increased. Poor people are not so poor as before, but they experience the differences and feel unhappy by them. The welfare state is clearly less so, than that state was some fifty years earlier.

Three generations of Britons have been followed from 1946 up to year 2000. In a conclusion on income and living standards, Dearden, Goodman and Saunders (2003) write:

> In conclusion, this chapter has demonstrated quite strikingly that, whilst living standards have, in general, risen steadily with each successive cohort, inequalities in income and wages have also increased. These findings alone represent a significant indicator of the changes in British society in the last decades of the twentieth century. However, it is also important to recall our finding that there was also a significant gradient in the incomes of cohort members according to their own parental background, as measured by their fathers' social class, and that this gradient appeared to have become *steeper* amongst more recent cohorts. Thus, not only has Britain become an increasingly unequal society, but the income achieved by the more recently born is more strongly linked to the social class position of their own parental generation.
>
> (p. 189)

A second important element: England and Wales have also reduced *the power of the judiciary*. The Home Office provides the courts with extensive statistics where each court can compare its own sentencing practice with what happens in all other courts in the country. Judges also receive various *guidelines*, not sentencing tables in the US style, but various forms of central guidance where precise tariffs are specified. And this process is in steady continuation. The *Guardian Weekly* (8 May 2003) describes a proposal from the Home Secretary the day before as this:

Life will mean life for:
• Multiple murders with a high degree of premeditation, involving abduction or sadistic conduct

- Murder of a child in similar circumstances
- Terrorist murderer
- Term will not apply to killers under 20

30-year minimum for killing:
- On-duty police or prison officer
- With gun or explosive
- On contract for other gain such as for racist, religious or sexist motives
- Adult for sadistic or sexual reasons
- Other multiple offences.

15 year minimum:
- Other murders by adults and all murders by children under 17

The *Guardian* reports that 'Senior lawyers were unhappy with the announcement . . . The Bar Council described it as constitutionally a leap in the dark' and said Mr Blunkett (the Home Secretary) was trying to 'institutionalise a grip of the executive around the neck of the judiciary'. The Howard League for Penal Reform said the package could increase the present 3,900 life sentence prisoners by 50 per cent.

Britain has also streamlined their system by establishing a position similar to that of a general procurator. They call him Solicitor General – a position with authority to keep everyone in line. It has also, for the higher courts, developed a system of professional prosecutors, and opened for appeals if prosecution so wants. Earlier, only the sentenced person could appeal. The official reason for much of this is often named 'consistency in sentencing'. But it can also be seen as a strong centralizing trend. I have met British judges that express the same complaints as some of the US judges; we are not to the same extent free to use discretion as we were earlier! Central authorities are distant from those to be sentenced, but close to politicians. Politicians are sensitive to punitive attitudes in the population and do also encourage such attitudes. Chances are great that a shift in the balance of power – from the judiciary to the politicians and their administrators – will open for more punitive measures.

Important changes have also taken place in the probation service in Great Britain. Once upon a time, the ruling idea here was to befriend the offender. Gradually, this has been changed. As in the US, probation is increasingly seen as an enforcement service. Probation has also been centralized; it is also here possible to control that the workers keep in line.

* * *

Penal systems are indicators of type of society. Changes in penal systems relate to changes within any particular society. The centralizing tendencies described in the penal system of England and Wales, the move from befriending offenders to enforcing control, and the strong growth in the prison population, are all probably linked to other basic changes. For the general political process within a country, it is important to be aware of what happens, and use that awareness for self-reflection.

5   State – or neighbours?

5.1 Icelandic blues?

Iceland is the country of Western Europe with the lowest number of prisoners. In summer 2002 they had one hundred prisoners, which means 35 per 100,000. They have one large prison with a capacity of 87 prisoners. But Icelanders do not like them that big, so happily enough they have also four small prisons with a capacity of between 6 and 14 persons. Erlendur Baldursson (2000) is from their prison administration. He tells that 'difficult prisoners have repeatedly been transferred from the largest prison to the smaller prisons, as a rule successfully'.

* * *

It is so easy to dismiss this experience. That little country Iceland, what happens there has no relevance for huge nations. I agree. On the other hand, some of these other nations also have lots of Iceland in the form of islands – inside their borders. First, in the form of small towns or cities. But large cities also have islands, inside. New York has several, Paris is said to consist of a great number of French villages, and London is also, as far as I can observe, a conglomeration of villages. In my little city, Oslo, I live in one. I moved to this island some 18 years ago, and have ever since been forced to reflect on why it is so extraordinarily good to live there.

Basically, because this part of the city by and large, but with exceptions such as myself, is a low income district. Simply, there is a large number of poor people around. From that follows four social facts:

1   A considerable amount of misery. The length of life for males here is 10 years shorter than in the West End. Living as single is more common here than elsewhere, so is it also to have problems with alcohol and drugs.

2   As a consequence of poverty, most people here do not have cars. From this follows that most people do not shop outside the local neighbourhood. There is no convenient transport available to super-markets outside the district borders. In addition, many will not have so much cash available that they can load up for several days. From this follows:

3   Local shops survive. There are not many parts of Oslo so filled with kiosks and small shops as in this area.

4   And one additional factor, a very important one: An extraordinary number of those living here are on welfare of one sort or another. This means they have more time available than most people have.

So, when Saturday arrives, and I should have been out skiing in the forest, that is how many natives are conditioned, then I am instead tempted out into the local streets, shopping, talking, or just being.

This has other consequences. This island is, as you might have gathered, a place for all sorts of people; some might be in official files with some sort of diagnosis. But in local neighbourhoods with much interaction, people do not remain *only* as diagnostic categories. People become characters: that man with the blind dog, the cigarette butt collector, the kind old lady, that youngster to keep away from . . .

This also means that we have less crime in such neighbourhoods than in the more affluent parts of the city. Of course, I do not, with this state-ment, say that less property disappears without the consent of the owner in my neighbourhood than in other neighbourhoods. Nor do I say that fewer people are bodily harmed than elsewhere. Probably there is more of both. What I do say is that these activities get another meaning on my island. We are not so scared, since we know our neighbours. And chances are great that we know some of the involved parties, or someone who knows some. This again means it does not feel quite so natural to use official designations such as 'theft' or 'violence'. Crime is a man-made phenomenon. Among people who know something about each other, it is less natural to use crime categories. We might dislike what they do, and attempt to hinder it. But we do not have quite the same need for the simple categories from penal law. And if applied, these labels do not stick to the same extent.

5.2 Extermination of primary relations

We know particularly well what follows when primary relations dissolve.

Some among us can still remember George Caspar Homans, that US navy officer with a voice trained to deafen storms. He turned anthropologist, and in his book from 1951 with the title *The Human Group*, he presented the beautiful horror story about the demise of 'Hilltown'. Once this was a town filled with important decision making. You could not be away from social life for long, or wrong decisions on important matters might be taken. It was a place with all the pleasures and pains of social life, a social system well suited for primary control. We know that primary control needs somebody close and concerned. If no one is there, the state will provide someone. Then to the sad end of the story: A railway appeared at the bottom of the Hill, giving easy access to the big world. The town converted into a sleepy suburb where internal life became of small consequence.

Forty-nine years later, Robert Putnam (2000) published his book *Bowling Alone*. From being socially outgoing, with many friends who often meet, deeply involved in civic life, the ordinary US person of today seems to be much more of a social isolate. From myriads of studies, Putnam compares generations. How did people 50 years old behave in 1955, compared to those of the same age in year 1995? He describes a clear trend towards increased social isolation. As a symbol of it all: Bowling is not so much a group activity any more, it has become an individual one. Bowling halls acquire huge TV screens to be watched while waiting for the next play. The adjacent restaurant is gone. So are the friends you used to meet there in between games. Now, after the game – which has become a competition against yourself – you drive home to another suburb, to a household where seven hours of TV watching is waiting – seven hours and two TV sets is the statistical norm for the country. Life in social networks is shrinking, while consumption of crime from the screen is increasing.

Putnam's analysis is met with criticism as to its importance for political life. His study is also to a surprising extent without a class perspective. Nonetheless, it is an essential finding that people do not meet people to the extent they once did. This means increased reliance on the media for describing what happens and what gives meaning to the occurrences. It also means greater dependence on the state to cope with these perceived dangers.

If I am acquainted with my neighbours and have some sort of network close to me, I have an easy time if some youngsters misbehave in my hallway. I can call for someone who might know some of them, or I can turn to the athletic neighbour one floor up – or perhaps better – I can ask for help from the little lady I know as particularly good at handling local conflicts.

But *without* a network, and with all the information on the increase of crime in mind, I would have locked the door and called the police.

I would thereby have created conditions both for encouraging unwanted behaviour, and for giving that unwanted behaviour the meaning of crime. Maybe I would also have encouraged conditions leading to an acceptance of an e-mail I received while I was working on this manuscript.

This was an irresistible offer launched under the title: 'Spy on your baby-sitter'. A few days later, I got the same offer under the title: 'Watch your teens or keep an eye on the babysitter.'

> it is a secret wireless camera used professionally by CIA, FBI and others . . . And here is how it works: A small camera hidden inside a lightbulb so inconspicuous no one will suspect they are being watched. You screw it into any lamp [even over the shower], it could be in a dark place it doesn't matter . . . Then you take the other piece and plug it into your VCR [or any type of TV, they say in other ads] and it is as if you were standing over the person with a video camera . . . The video signal 'wraps around' the power line, completely separate from the AC voltage. This is a security no home or office should be without.

But there are other dangers. Another e-mail gives comfort: The subject line is 'Stop child molesters', and the offer is to get access to a database with more than 50,000,000 criminal files. And we learn:

> The odds are great that one or more of these dangerous criminals may be living in your neighbourhood. Approximately 200,000 convicted rapists are required to be registered in America at any one time. Many are repeat offenders.

Access to the database of sex offenders is free of charge, but access to the file for the 50 million costs 10 dollars.

5.3 Trivial truths

And what do we do and say, we, the legions of social scientists around? We know, as a profession, some of the consequences of all this. But we do not tell, not often, not strongly, and particularly, not concretely, with examples and detail. What we have to say is so much against the spirit of our time.

We know about city planning. A large shopping centre is projected outside an old city. Gains: Reduced unemployment during the construction period, increased income to the construction firms and later to the firms running the centres, and probably also a greater assortment of goods and improved conditions for parking. But then the penal costs: Increased number of arrests for shop-lifting, and also the social death of the old city in the neighbourhood, leading to an increased amount of unwanted behaviour. Police and guards become necessary as functional alternatives to the missing counters and the neighbourhood shops.

So, we can say: Dissolve the supermarkets. And let all shops have a counter between customers and commodities.

Or, as an alternative to the methods of the New York subway police, we can say: To reduce penal costs, let no bus or streetcar run without a conductor. Social control carried out by a person who does not give the situation the meaning of having crime control as its primary purpose leads to an increased feeling of security among all passengers. It creates a quieter atmosphere, more co-operation from other passengers and less use of force. But, of course, economic costs: Salaries to conductors minus costs for ticket machines, electronic surveillance, and increase in payment from those who usually do not pay.

Or we might turn really radical and say: Poverty is a relative phenomenon. Reduce the wealth of the rich, and the poor would not be that poor.

We know a lot, if questioned by journalists or others. But, of course, we also know the journalists will not be particularly interested and not come back. They will turn to more useful criminologists, not to free eggheads. I will return to this theme in Chapter 8.

5.4 Old-fashioned Russia

I have the privilege of living close to Eastern Europe. Norway and Russia have a joint border up in the north. And we have had no wars – except for Norwegian invasions in Viking times. But there is more to it than that. I feel at home going east. This is not because of a similarity there with my present living in my home country. It is more like coming back to the days of my grandmother. It is not only in Russia this happens. So is it also in Poland, in Hungary and in many of the other Eastern European countries.

Why?

I have no solid explanation, again only a vague hunch. Perhaps it is due to communism. But not as stated in the old propaganda, not due to the effects of communism as we were told about in their fairytales back in time about workers' paradise and all that. Not because of the transformation of some of these societies that took place after 1918. And particularly not because of the efficiency in the changes. On the contrary, it is because of the *inefficiency*. Capitalism was able to change Western countries, change them into their present monolithic form, change their forms as well as their basic values. State communism of the Eastern type was also able to change their societies. They changed the type of government, and exchanged the incumbents of power positions. With enormous human and material costs, they improved living conditions for many. They modernized the material structures. But they were not very good in modernizing the human soul.

5.5 Societies with more than one leg

Even in the middle of the cold war, there existed some professional contacts between the East and West of Europe. We received some official visitors from Soviet criminology in Norway in the early 1960s, and returned the visit in 1968. From then onwards, exchanges were frequent. A book of mine – *Limits to Pain* (Christie 1981) – was published in the USSR in 1985; I think it was the first 'Western' criminology published there. This made contacts more legitimate and opened up for further interaction with the Russians, and by that legitimizing fact also with their colleagues in other East European countries.

I give this little sketch of background to establish some sort of credibility to my next point, which simply is an elaboration of the points above: These countries were, and still to some extent are, so remarkably old-fashioned. Of course, it is like that. These were societies functioning at a much lower technical and material level than in the West. Their populations were living under a political system where the state was supposed to provide the material goods needed for life. But that state was not particularly reliable in delivery. And it was a one-party system. Political opposition was a dangerous matter. People did not want to talk to you in the streets, visits in private homes might be a dangerous endeavour – for the host. Leaving Eastern Europe by train was an unpleasant experience. Armed inspectors entered, scrutinizing the luggage compartments; maybe someone had attempted to escape their state, flashlights under the trains, dogs, and of course guns. It was like leaving a prison.

A scarcity of commodities, and an abundance of state control. No wonder many looked for other systems of protection!

I brought a granddaughter to Russia quite recently. It was for a seminar in Astrakhan, a long journey with ample time for talks with the participants. Most encounters had the same beginning: My granddaughter, 14 years old, was warmly greeted, so nice to meet a Norwegian girl. And then, with certainty, a few seconds later came the fatal question: What was she planning to do in her life, what sort of study, and what sort of work was she preparing for? My granddaughter looked at me in despair, until she got accustomed to the repeated question. She was an ordinary Norwegian teenager. Life is open. She would finish her compulsory education, maybe a year of travel abroad, maybe university, maybe first some years of ordinary work to earn money . . . Then, perhaps, some years of study, but this would certainly not be a choice for grandfathers to interfere with. 'I have with one exception never got such a question at home,' she told me after the first cross-examinations. But I felt the blame from my Russian colleagues. They thought of me as a bad grandfather. Careless in the extreme. With such a clever and lively granddaughter – and he has not been able to put her on the right track for a vocation!

I ought to have been prepared. For years, I have been struck by the survival ability of the intelligentsia in Eastern Europe. In these societies, constructed to benefit the working class, I was rarely able to meet academic people who had not one or two academicians as parents, and often also as grandparents. Probably, but here I am on less safe ice, probably this is only a special case of what had happened in other segments of Russian society. In scarcity, and under daily control of a powerful state, families, and family values, became of greater importance than in the West. Under scarcity, generations are forced into proximity. For a young couple – she might be pregnant – the only solution is a room or a part of a room in the parents' dwelling. The family has small children and both mother and father need paid work to survive. Grandparents become a treasure, just as children are to them when the old age pension fails to appear. Or the *datcha*, the little summer house so dear to those that had one, a fortune for the extended family, a place to be for the kids, a place for the production of vegetables for them all. To be an outsider in such a system means serious danger. Social capital has material realities.

The dark side of the one-party state pushed in the same direction. Informers are essential in such systems, as was so clearly documented in the Stasi archives after the collapse of the Federal Republic of Germany. You never could know, for certain, who the informers were. Probably (but not certainly) they were not in the close family. Ivo Moszny, a perceptive sociologist from Brno in the Czech Republic, has in conversations and lectures repeatedly pointed to this phenomenon. I met him during the 'Prague Spring', a short period with decreased political oppression. When that peculiar spring had passed, he was in a way rescued. He got a position as a janitor at his old university. Today, he is the Dean of the same faculty. Once, in an old Norwegian bus, a group of Scandinavian criminologists travelled to Vienna via Poland and what was then Czechoslovakia. This was in the period when he still was a janitor. He gave a remarkable lecture, inside our bus, outside of the ears of state control. It was precisely on the importance of the family for resistance against totalitarian states that he spoke.

Hundreds of small lagoons for a life alternative to the one controlled by the state were constructed. The family was one. But so also was the culture of the past, the heritage, the large novels, the music, the poetry. To live in scarcity might also give room for an alternative life. This is one explanation for the cultural interest one also meets today in Russia and in some of the neighbouring states. But maybe there is more to this interest than just being a refuge against a totalitarian regime. Maybe the pronounced cultural/aesthetic interest is a deep feature of what it is to be Russian. Maybe it will survive material affluence. That crucial test is happily enough not close to us in time.

*   *   *

But the Soviet heritage is not that far back in time. Let me turn to that.

5.6 Those Polish students

I was invited to lecture in Poland, and used some of the themes above: The need for informal social networks, the need for knowing your neighbours, and the need for primary control as an alternative to state control. I met blank faces. Of course I met blank faces. Trained to distrust your neighbour, conditioned to situations where that neighbour might be a spy for the system, it might all come back, why establish ties that might prove dangerous? This is one of the serious costs of having been trained into life in a one-party state.

These same costs are also clear when attempts are made to introduce mediation or restorative justice in Eastern Europe. They have had their quota of it. They have had house committees or neighbourhood committees. Or they have had workers' courts in the factories – no more of this, thank you!

Again, it is easy to understand. They had it all, but were strictly politically governed. Those who decided were perhaps mediators, but they were also party members. The great interest in alternative conflict solutions in the West is met with considerably less enthusiasm in Eastern Europe, and with good historical reasons.

But this might also be an important experience for Western attempts to curb the state by introducing civil ways of handling conflicts. Let me turn to this theme.

6   No punishment

6.1 Two types of justice

We know the picture: Females gathering at the water fountain or at natural meeting places along the river. Here they come, often every day at the same time. Fetch the water, wash the clothes, and exchange information and evaluations. The point of departure for their conversations will often be concrete acts and situations. These are described, compared with similar occurrences in the past and evaluated; was it right or wrong what happened, was it beautiful or ugly, was it a sign of strength or weakness? Males will often do the same, at their places of meeting. Slowly, but far from always, some common understanding of the occurrences might emerge. This is a process whereby norms are created through interaction. Let us call it *horizontal* justice, created by persons with considerable equality brought about by closeness. Of course, not complete equality. Some have better clothes than others, some are from better families, some have more wit. But compared to what now follows, they are equals. And their decisions are based on being part of a process.

* * *

Horizontal justice has three major characteristics:

1   Decisions are *locally* anchored. How cases are solved in villages far away is of limited interest. What matters is here and now, compared with the past, and with concern for the future. This can lead to inequality between districts; the 'same' act can be evaluated differently in district A than in district B and C. But the opinion inside each of these districts might unanimously be that justice has been achieved in their particular area.
2   Questions of relevance are handled in a radically different way from what happens in the legal system. Relevance is seen as a central concern, but in situations with horizontal justice as one *without*

pre-defined solutions. Relevance is established through the process itself. Relevant is what the participants find relevant. A minimum degree of consensus on relevance must be created among all interested parties. That Kari 15 years back in time was humiliated by Per, might be seen as of considerable importance by all interested discussants when Kari's little sister has now covered Per's little brother with tar and thereafter rolled him in feathers.

3   At the water well, compensation becomes more important than retribution. This is related to several structural elements in small-scale societies. Such societies are often relatively egalitarian. Not necessarily in the meaning that all are equal in wealth or prestige, but in the meaning that *if* conflicts appear, parties will move into alliances with their relatives and friends and thus mobilize until they become somehow equal to their opponents. Many such societies also exist far away from external authorities with power at their disposal. This means that they themselves will have to cope with the conflicts. This is a situation where the participants know each other from far back in time, and also know that they will have to live together in the future. They cannot do as modern people do, just break off relationships and move to another social system when conflicts loom. Punishments are particularly dysfunctional in such systems. Punishment – infliction of pain intended as pain – means moving towards civil war in fragile systems. With a distant external authority, with nowhere else to move, and with no superiority of power, compensation rather than pain becomes the natural answer.

*   *   *

Then the other picture: Moses, down from the mountain. Under his arm he carried the rules, engraved in stone, dictated to him by one even higher up than the top of that mountain. Moses was only a messenger, the people – the populace – were the receivers, controlled from far above. Much later, Jesus and Mohammed functioned according to the same principles. These are classical cases of what here will be designated as vertical justice.

In the case of Moses and his vertical justice, the situation is different from one of horizontal justice. With rules engraved in stone, an idea of the existence of general validity is created. Equal cases have to be treated equally and according to the rules. But cases are never equal, if everything is taken into consideration. Of course not. Therefore, *everything can not be taken into consideration* in formal law. It becomes necessary to eliminate most of the factors surrounding any act to be able to create cases that can be presumed to be similar or equal. This process is called eliminating what is *irrelevant*. But what is irrelevant is a matter of values. To create equality, it is therefore necessary to create rules for irrelevancy. It is a dogmatically decided irrelevance – as lay people so often experience when their lawyers forbid them to bring up in court what they believe is their best argument. This is what we train law students to know and apply. This type of justice is reached by establishing limitations on what can be taken into account, otherwise equality could not be established in this setting. This is in sharp contrast to horizontal justice where the question of relevance is decided among the participants in the process.

With vertical justice, and the social distance implied in that process, there is also created a situation that opens up for the application of punishment, for pain intended as pain.

Modernity means to a large extent a life amidst people we do not know and never will come to know. This is a situation where penal law can be applied with great ease. Penal law and modern time suit each other.

6.2 The growth of formal law

Every second year, a new edition of a peculiar book comes to my office. It is a book published by the Faculty of Law at the University of Oslo. The book is red, large and voluminous, even printed on 'Bible paper'. In 1930, the book contained 2,099 pages; in 2002, the number of pages had increased to 3,111. This is the book that contains all valid Norwegian laws from 1687 and up to the present. No lawyer will be without a new edition of this book. Students of law will often carry the book under their arm – the book has some of the same symbolic function for law students as the stethoscope for students of medicine.

In addition to laws in books, these days there are also the electronically conveyed messages. With the morning coffee, the last legal decisions can be called up on the screen by all the legal experts who are connected to a legal database. And they will all soon *have* to be connected if they want to be taken seriously. The courts are under continuous electronic upgrading in all highly industrialized countries. In the case of the penal courts, the sentencing tables of the US type will soon be outdated. Information on offender and offence can be fed into the electronic system, and out come details of the 'profile' – the range of sentences in 'similar' cases, not obligatory to follow, but yet persuasive examples of how other judges act. From carved in stone to a diagram on what is a normal sentence on a screen. The electronic revolution has not created egalitarian justice, but a pyramidal one.

In the meantime, the water wells and a great number of other arenas for informal discussions are abolished, even though coffee shops to some extent have taken over. Disappeared also have many of the old villages. But a new type of village has recently appeared. What happens there illustrates some of the strength in the horizontal participatory justice system.

6.3 The global village

The females at the water well would often look differently at much of this. It was as if they were not so sure of their classifications. What is what, and who is who? But they are not there, any more. Instead, a new type of users of mediation has grown in strength and importance. These are the large economic enterprises.

It is often said that in modern societies the village is dead. Gone. Just an empty shell to sleep in. Our destiny is life in the megatown, a life among strangers. That is right. But also wrong. The villages have died. All but the global village.

If we want to study a village of importance today, we must not go to the countryside, but to the very centre of countries. We must go to the city. Literally. We must go to the City of London, Wall Street, or to some of the inner districts of Tokyo or Singapore, perhaps even to Oslo. Arriving there, we must look for some of the best-protected buildings, and then within these, try to get access to some of the major enterprises occupying these premises. In my country, it might be one of the major oil companies, or even better, one of the large law firms. Entering their premises is similar to entering a hut in an African village.

How can I utter such an absurdity? For three good reasons. But as I list them, you will have to accept that, in what follows, I have had to simplify and give an ideal-typical description.

First, those living in the modern hut are *linked* to their neighbours in ways having functional similarities with the old ones: By telephones, sometimes integrated with TV pictures, by telephone-conferences, often with participants with oceans between them, or faxes or e-mails. Linked together, and with a common cultural landscape from reading the *Financial Times*, the *Wall Street Journal* or *The Economist*.

Second, they are *glued* to each other, just as the old-fashioned villagers were. There is no other globe available. They live there with the understanding that they will have to remain, or leave for the desert.

Third, the external authorities are far away, and with limited power. One modern law firm might have a larger legally trained staff than the whole Ministry of Justice and the Ministry of the Interior put together. They know more of law, and dispose more resources than their rulers.

This, then, also makes them similar to the old-fashioned villagers when conflicts loom. They have nowhere else to go, so they continue the relationships. But since they have no external authority to turn to for protection they are again forced into ordinary village behaviour. They must solve the conflicts by civil means. We know from personal experience, or from social anthropology, that attempts to punish others in the village mean breaking off relationships. It is a call for war. Conflicts in villages without external authority and where people intend to remain, such conflicts will most often take a form whereby the parties create coalitions to muster some sort of balance of strength. After this groundwork is done, they meet and work towards civil solutions. If wrong acts have been performed, compensation to the victim, not pain to the offender, becomes the major answer where relationships are to continue. As for the villagers everywhere, so also for General Electric.

Penal law is a perfect instrument for certain purposes, but clumsy for others. It is one where we eliminate many concerns, and it is one based on dichotomies – all or nothing, guilty or not guilty. In many situations we are half guilty. If that half guilt is seen in the light of earlier misdeeds of the other party – or her or his associates – an opening is given for compromise. Civil solutions are more integrative solutions striving to preserve the social system as a body of interacting individuals.

In analogy with what happens in village law, lawyers in the global village will most often consider the totality of situations and look for peaceful compromises and compensation rather than the use of swords. They will, as peacemakers and mediators everywhere, be highly regarded and, in our culture, highly paid. Without a high reputation, they will, in certain types of villages, have trouble creating peace. They will therefore guard their honour both against political involvement and against clients of low regard. High salary is a corollary to high regard. In addition to money and prestige, they have probably also more fun than other kinds of lawyers. In their global village, inside the limits of their economic-administrative system, they are back to working with totalities. They have the fun of old-fashioned tribal members in finding out about the law, participating in finding solutions all parties can live with, and thereafter the satisfaction of creating peace inside their system. They are engaged in a holistic activity directed towards peace, in contrast to a specialized one directed towards war.

The paradox is that, as these lawyers are enjoying their global village, they are so often causing destruction of the remaining local villages. Their decisions on the economy are part of the driving forces in the international development of industrialization. Their activities in their global village are one of the key elements in the process of modernity. Their activities create the conditions where another kind of legal personnel is called for, a kind in extreme contrast to the civil one suited for conflicts at the water well.

* * *

So, what have I described so far?

I have described two ways of coping with conflicts, the way of Moses, and the way of the women at the water well. And I have said there is growth and expansion in *both* solutions. Growth in penal law, but also growth in the interest for mediation.

6.4 Abolish punishment?

In discussions on penal matters, a major position is called *abolitionism*.

The abolitionists raise questions like: What logic, and ethic, makes it so certain that punishment has priority over peacemaking? You lost an eye due to my deplorable behaviour, but I will give you my house. You hurt me with your crazy driving, but I have forgiven you. Punishment is intended pain. Has the intended delivery of pain advantages as an instrument for restoring broken values? Has such pain advantages, and therefore priority, over reconciliation, restoration, and forgiveness? I agree with the position behind these questions, but cannot follow the abolitionists all the way.

The most radical among them want to eliminate penal law and formal punishment altogether. But there are several major problems with that position if followed to the extreme.

The first is a concern for those who do not wish to participate in a process of reconciliation or in reaching a possible agreement. Some offenders do not have the ability, nor would they dare to look the victim in the eye, let alone ask for forgiveness; they panic and want an impersonal court procedure. Neither would some victims consider reconciliation; they prefer the offender being punished. In both cases, a criminal legal process commences. A civil conflict-solving process can hardly be considered in a modern state without a criminal law solution being available as a possible alternative. This might result in one person being forgiven in a civil case, while another person is punished. But it cannot be against the code of ethics that some, though not all, receive forgiveness. Those punished encounter what they would have faced if restoration did not exist. Probably, those punished will receive a bit less. If forgiveness exists as a viable alternative in some cases, this would possibly reduce the severity of punishments in general within the system.

Another major concern if punishments were completely abolished, is that reconciliation processes could degenerate. The offender, or his close relatives, might in despair promise too much in order to turn matters in a more favourable direction. The arbitrator, the mediator or participants in a circle must stop this, and might be forced to return such a case to the penal courts. Or the offender might be exposed to too strong pressure from the other party. There are instances from small communities where the men dominate the conflict-solving body and where the abused women are subjected to continued suppression.

For conflicts at the state level, the same objection can be raised. Laura Nader (2002) expresses it like this:

> Fine-grained fieldwork indicates how coercive harmony operates to silence disputing indigenous peoples who speak or act angrily.
>
> (p. 127)
>
> . . .
>
> It began to look very much as if ADR [Alternative Dispute Resolution] were a pacification scheme, an attempt on the part of powerful interests in law and in economics to stem litigation by the masses, disguised by the rhetoric of an imaginary litigation explosion.
>
> (p. 144)

In enthusiasm for mediation, it is important not to forget that rituals and arrangements in penal courts might have important protective functions. When tensions run high, maybe even immediate violence threatens, the solemn and also often utterly tedious and dull rituals in the penal apparatus might have a calming effect. Court procedures might make certain situations of conflict bearable, just as church rituals – or nowadays the fast developing 'human ethical rituals' – make it possible to endure the suffering at a funeral for a beloved one.

A special situation is created when an individual stands against an organization. It might be the shoplifter against the big firm, the graffiti making youngster against the municipality, or the passenger who did not pay against the subway system. The point here is not necessarily the inequality in power, but that one party will be a representative for a big organization. It might be a representative with a large amount of routine, but a limited amount of personal interest in the conflict. In contrast, the other party might represent herself or himself for the first time. Our official system for mediation in Norway is soaked with shoplifters, cases particularly unsuited for mediation. The system for mediation might easily be perverted into juvenile courts in disguise. Høigård (2002, pp. 288–93) has a highly relevant critique of this development in her book on graffiti, *Street Galleries*. What goes on in these mediation boards is, in her view, punishment of children.

An exception would be if the mediators on the boards were able to include the top management of the big firm or of the subway system or the municipality. In that case, it would be possible to raise questions about how the shops are organized, if the temptations in the shop are exhibited in a way that make them close to irresistible to youngsters, and if the shop in order to increase profit has far too few sales attendants around. Or the question might be raised if the graffiti on the wall was not more beautiful and/or interesting than the huge advertisements for underwear? Such meetings might be very useful for the social system in general. But to get them going is probably utopian.

A third case for penal procedure is a situation in which there is no actual victim. Perhaps a belief has been offended against. Some people might curse God or Allah in nations where this is considered a serious sin. Or perhaps there is a need to regulate what some people are doing to themselves and their own bodies. Action against the use of drugs is at present the dominant example.

And then comes the more trivial concern that some simple regulations would ultimately need support. Some drivers insist on driving at the speed of their choice. Civil measures, such as the withdrawal of a driving licence or the impounding of a vehicle, could be attempted, but are not always sufficient. Punishment should remain as a last resort.

For some, none of the above concerns are of importance. Still they would punish. They will say: Society has to do it. Independently of any utility or practical use of punishment, certain acts are so terrible that the perpetrator(s) must receive the vengeance of society. This would be their claim.

6.5 A winter night

Forty thousand citizens of Oslo took to the streets the very same week I was writing this chapter. It was on the first day of February, and it was dark and bitterly cold. A strong northern wind swept through the streets, the temperature was −13°C but nonetheless, it was warming to be there.

Benjamin was the reason for it all. Some of his friends gave speeches, so also did the Prime Minister. A young woman sang. Thereafter followed a solemn procession through the streets. Benjamin had been killed three days earlier. He had just turned 15. Knifed by three young people with some sympathies for Nazi ideology. Enough is enough was the dominant mood of the country. Benjamin had black skin. A year earlier he had, on national TV, condemned Norwegian racism. That might have been one of the reasons for his death.

The procession was a manifestation of common values, and also an example of the new types of funeral rites coming into being – as flowers for Diana, candles on graves, or at the places where terrible events have occurred. Public participation encouraged by and broadly covered by the media.

But then the question: Is this enough?

Much has already been done to prevent the spread of Nazi ideology and the establishment of Nazi organizations. The state gives money to youth activists to help to get young people involved in Nazi groups to retreat from these settings, and return to normal life. Parents are active, schools likewise, and researchers attempt to get close to the Nazi groups to understand their behaviour and their motivation.[1]

But again, is this enough? Two young men and a woman have been found guilty.[2] Is it possible to think in terms of restorative justice in such a case? The value of a human life has been infringed upon. And not only this. The act has been carried out by persons that at least initially might have thought the act was a positive one, a move to fight back the invasion of a less valuable culture, or maybe even a less valuable race. Would I still insist that this also is a case for restorative justice?

*   *   *

There are other difficult cases. In Norway recently, the entire population was shocked by the murder of two small girls who were going to swim in a little lake in a forest somewhere in the south of the country. They were sexually molested and killed. Two young men were found guilty and given long sentences. One of them seemed to laugh when he left the court. The population was outraged, and so was I.

Nonetheless, let us try to imagine another end to the story. What would have happened if mediation had been arranged and the relatives, after a long process, said: You killed our children, but we have forgiven you. With our present knowledge of your past life history, and with an acceptance of the sincerity of your deep remorse, we have forgiven you. We know what your future will be if you have to spend years in prison, therefore we beg the authorities to release you. What would have happened if this had been said by the relatives, and followed up by the authorities?

I have no doubts about this being a solution in accordance with deep roots in our morality. But at the same time I do not have any doubt that it is completely unreasonable to *expect* this to happen, let alone to demand that the next of kin to those murdered should take part in a negotiation process that could possibly lead to an end result like this. It is perfectly understandable and morally above blame for the next of kin to choose punishment for the offender. But *if* mediation took place, could we then conceive of a situation where the case *ended* there – ended with forgiveness? Why should it be obvious that the case still belonged to the prosecutor and prison authorities?

If all the victims, and all the relatives of those who could no longer talk, had claimed that forgiveness should reign, then, maybe, maybe, a sociologist would take Emile Durkheim in hand and argue that for the sake of the social cohesion of that particular society it might be necessary to let punishment follow the disgusting acts. But the possibility of such a forgiveness from the parties involved is so distant that this kind of warning is as realistic as a warning of the breakdown of the oil market because most people have found it morally right to drop any use of private cars. But if it happened, I would be at the side of those parents that asked for forgiveness. The whole process of finding out what had happened, the determination of guilt, the quest for forgiveness, and then the act of forgiving – it would all be a powerful exposure of terrible, close to unbelievable, horrible, gruesome acts. The exposure of it all would represent a powerful distancing from those acts, at the same time as the act of forgiveness would take care of another equally important set of fundamental values in our society.

* * *

But would that be justice? In extreme cases, children are sexually abused in a horrible way, then killed. It cannot be right to let the guilty ones get away with words only? But the opposite position might also be a wrong answer. The punishment can never be equal to the wrong done. As Giertsen (2003) writes, here in my translation:

> Punishment is a symbolic expression, it can not become equal to the crime in the relation one to one, and cannot be used as a measure-stick expressing the value of the victim. Punishment is first and foremost a statement that an act has damaged an important value, a value that must be re-established.
>
> (p. 13)

Punishment cannot be equal to damage. Relatives might say: He who killed was only sentenced to twelve years, while my boy lost his whole life. That is not right! And they are also right, so far. But they are reasoning in a way that would lead society into unacceptable conditions. If we want to preserve humanity, it is not a question of simple retribution. The lost son cannot be brought back; a similar harm would be to take the culprit's life under conditions equal to his way of acting. Our ethic must have a broader perspective. If punishment is to take place, this punishment must represent the totality of our values.

Victims, and victim movements, will often feel deeply hurt when their sufferings are not reflected in the punishment on a basis of one to one. This will often be expressed as sharp criticism of the courts, a criticism eagerly brought to the surface in the media and from there to the politicians.

How to handle this situation?

There are no other ways than the usual: counter-arguments, exchange of ideas, attempts at clarification. Choice of penal policy is a cultural question. It is not a question of instinctive actions and re-actions. It is an area filled with deep moral questions. It is an area for novelists, playwrights, artists – and for all citizens. It is not only for experts, of course not. But it is not only for victims either. It must be a chorus of voices, introducing a forest of concerns, partly concerns that are not easily digested, and also to a large extent not in harmony. The more the field is seen as a cultural one, the less room remains for the simplified solutions.

6.6 Minimalism

I hope the reasoning up to this point makes it clear that abolitionism, in its purified form, is not an attainable position. We cannot abolish the penal institution totally. But I have also, I hope, in the foregoing chapters been able to show that we can go a long way in that direction. Crime does not exist as a natural phenomenon. Crime is just one among several possible ways of looking at deplorable acts. We are free to choose, and the variation in punishment levels over time in individual states and also between states is an illustration of that freedom.

In this situation, what comes close to my heart might be called *minimalism*.[3] This is close to the abolitionist position, but accepts that in certain cases, punishment is unavoidable. Both abolitionists and minimalists take undesirable acts as their point of departure, not acts defined as crimes. And they ask how these acts can be dealt with. Can compensating the injured party help to handle the case, or establishing a truth commission, or helping the offender to ask for forgiveness? A minimalist position opens up choice. By taking the point of departure in the whole sequence of events leading to the undesirable action, punishment becomes one, but only one, among several options. To let the analysis stem from conflicts, rather than from crime, opens up a liberating perspective. It means that we are not captured in a 'penal necessity', but are free to choose.

Good – and bad. It takes away the rigidity in seeing punishment as an absolute obligation, but forces us to give some reasons for our choice of punishment versus non-punishment. Let us, in what follows, test the possibilities of the minimalist position on some catastrophes of our time.

7 Answers to atrocities

7.1 Blind, deaf and without memory

It is obvious that none of us could have survived with a memory of all we might have remembered. It would result in overload. We do not register all the writings on those walls we pass. And if we register them, we remember only a fragment. We are highly selective in what we see, in what we store, and in what we recall. What is abortion to the doctor might be perceived as killing by the priest. To some women it might be a moment of great relief, to others the utmost of sin, hidden behind stone walls in the mind.[1] We perceive selectively, we remember selectively, we recall selectively. We construct.

I was a child in an occupied country during World War II. I did the usual things. Followed the rules: Never fraternize with a German soldier or a Norwegian Nazi member. Nevertheless, I cannot remember anything from what happened when the Jews were deported. I cannot remember one single comment about it in my generally patriotic circles. The ordinary Norwegian police apprehended the Jews. Since they were so many, one hundred ordinary taxis were used for transportation to the ship that brought most of them to their death in German concentration camps. I suppose the drivers soon forgot this episode in their lives. When the few survivors came home from the camps, they came to a country that to some extent had forgotten that they had ever been there. Much of their property was also gone. It was not until 1996 that they – or mostly their children and grandchildren – got some decent compensation.

Silence is one of the answers to atrocities. Silence, because there is nobody around to listen. Isolation of the victim is one of the major features of social systems where illegitimate violence is applied. The mechanism can be observed in cases of battered women. Husbands in such cases tend to isolate wife and children, see to it that they have no close friends or relatives nearby. Kids are not allowed to bring friends home. There is nobody to tell. Or maybe nothing to tell. The dinner was not ready when the man came home that day or the meat not quite tender. Maybe he had reasons for his anger? Her intellectual need for an explanation is directed towards her own deficiencies and silences her protest. To change this, it is essential that she comes out of isolation and gets access to an audience that will not strengthen her man's definition of the situation.

So also in concentration camps. Those unable to see themselves as enemies of the oppressors seemed to be worse off than the militant opponents supporting a cause. Those unable had no explanation, nothing to tell themselves, except that it all was a terrible misunderstanding.

Most prisoners struggled to break the silence, to convey the truth to those outside the camps. The milk bucket from the ghetto in Lodz is a moving example. Lodz is the big industrialized city roughly halfway between Krakow and Warsaw. Throughout all the turmoil in the ghetto, a newspaper was printed there every day, in three copies. A few days before the last major transport left in 1944, one copy of all the volumes was hidden in a bucket, buried, regained after the war, and then published in the terrible/wonderful book by Lucjan Dobroszycki (1984): *The Chronicle of the Lodz Ghetto 1941–1944*. Here the victims got a voice.

7.2 Justice done

Not far from Krakow is Auschwitz and, next to that, one of the major death camps, Birkenau. Where the railway tracks end in Lager Birkenau, a gallows was raised after World War II. Here they hanged the Commander.

I have never been able to understand it. One life against one and a half million! One broken neck against all those suffocated, starved to death, or plainly killed in that camp. To me, the execution of the commander became a sort of denigration of the 1.5 million victims. Their worth became, for each of them, 1.5 millionth of the worth of the Commander.

But what else could be done? So asked my Polish colleagues when I, far back in time, revealed my doubts. And I had no answer, except this: Maybe a trial had to be carried out. Day after day survivors would have to reveal what happened. All sorts of victims would have to express their despair, rage and wish for vengeance. The Commander would also express his position, his reasons then, and now, in front of the survivors and his judges.

But then, for the judge, if he was a free judge and not only an executioner hired by the rulers, what should he in the end decide?

One possibility, and that would be my preference, would be that the judge should have spoken as follows to the Camp Commander: You have clearly done it. You have administered the death of more than a million human beings. You are guilty. Your acts are morally repulsive to an extent beyond what can be imagined. We have heard it. Everyone in the civilized world will get to know about your horrible acts carried out at this horrible place. No more can be said and done. Go away in shame.

But of course, I know that could not happen. I had, in the beginning of the 1960s, long talks with Professor Batawia in Warsaw. He was professor in forensic psychiatry, and had carried out long conversations with the commander of one of the large concentration camps. I have forgotten which one, most likely it was Rudolf Höss. We compared notes. I had worked in the same field, interviewing guards who tortured and killed in the *Nacht und Nebel* (Night and Fog) camps in the north of Norway. We found that we had two common experiences. First, neither of us had met any monsters from the camps. Bad news for those hoping to find beasts behind the atrocities; by and large they are not there. Second, neither the Polish, nor the Norwegian society was particularly interested in getting acquainted with our results. Batawia was flatly forbidden to publish; my small articles were ignored. It was not until a new generation had grown up that I was asked to publish the whole report as a book (Christie 1952/74). With closeness to the atrocities, it was revenge that was asked for, not analysis.

7.3 The execution of an idea

Nonetheless, they might have been right, those who hanged the commander. They not only hanged the commander, but a whole system. His broken neck symbolized a broken idea. It was the Nazi ideology that was hanged on the gallows. Societies need clear and fast answers when their most fundamental values have been under attack, as they were in the Nazi era.

I agree, of course I agree, how could I not.

7.4 A block against understanding

Nonetheless, in a little corner of my sociological conscience lurk some doubts. We kill the commander, yes. We even killed the major initiators after Nuremberg. We exterminated the evil ideas and their major carriers, swiftly, unanimously. We make it crystal clear that certain acts – genocide and the extermination of what they called unwanted minorities – are crimes so far out that no mercy is possible. But still: Do we thereby hit the whole target? By hanging the commander and also those bosses in Nuremberg, a good feeling of accomplishment was created; vengeance, often called justice, was carried out. But at the same time, the discussion of ideas and interests behind the Nazi period, and also related phenomena still alive, was effectively cut off.

The commander was guilty and from a retributive perspective he certainly deserved his destiny. But nonetheless, at the very same time, he also functioned as a scapegoat, as did his chiefs who were hanged in Nuremberg. Behind them were some untamed forces protected by the penal actions against their carriers. Atrocities, when met with individual punishments, might prevent the development of a more complex and therefore more helpful understanding of these forces and of the phenomena in general. It was not until 1989 that we got into the deeper layers of the understanding of the concentration camps with Zygmunt Bauman's book *Modernity and the Holocaust*.

By hanging commanders, and while the judges in Nuremberg focused on finding personal guilt for the atrocities, other phenomena were left in peace, left to grow. Three themes were *not* discussed in Nuremberg:

• Dresden
• Hiroshima and Nagasaki
• The Gulags

Dresden was made into a no-town in less than 24 hours, with at least 135,000 victims. It has later been difficult to find rational military reasons for their extinction. But it never became a theme in Nuremberg, in the court of the victorious.

Hiroshima and Nagasaki were made into graveyards with one atom bomb to each town. The reasons behind these mass killings of civilians seem unclear. But no one – even if they tried – could have raised the question in Nuremberg or before any other international court. It has been difficult to find rational military reasons for what happened. A better founded hypothesis seems to be that the dropping of the bombs was intended as a sign of warning to the USSR, a glorious introduction to the cold war.

And then there are the Gulags. Of course they could not be discussed in Nuremberg with a prominent Russian among the judges. But while they decided on death in Nuremberg, the Gulags bulged.

* * *

By hanging the individuals most closely related to the atrocities, we re-establish certain standards. We teach everybody a lesson. Mass killers will end on the gallows. Maybe we are preventing other people from going into the service of evil forces.

These are the conventional arguments for all severe punishments. And I think they have even less validity here than in more ordinary cases. Perpetrators of this type of evil act see themselves as servants of states surrounded by aggressors. Or their self-conception is to be just functionaries, as Adolph Eichman in his office. Or they see themselves as soldiers in an inevitable and also just war of a type their opponents call terror. In my country, we shot the chief traitor Vidkun Quisling after World War II. It is not reasonable to think that this will influence the next potential traitor. The situation will be different; the cause will be different. And the next person in similar circumstances will, while he acts, see himself as an obvious winner. The bandits on the other side are the ones who will be brought to court.

7.5 If impunity reigns

But, of course, I do also know what would have happened if the commander of Birkenau and some of the Nazi bosses had not been killed. The anger around them was overwhelming and uncontrollable. In some concentration camps, the guards were torn into pieces on the very day of liberation.

The urge for vengeance has to be respected in such circumstances. But it then has to be tamed, channelled into the penal law apparatus, and calmed by being placed in the hands of the state. If impunity reigns, peace cannot be re-established.

This is a major argument for formal penal action. It is a good one. But it points to a solution with severe costs attached, costs that often appear much later in the life of a nation. Let me illustrate with experiences from my own country, Norway.

7.6 Quisling

During World War II, the word 'quisling' was widely used as a synonym for 'traitor'. In Norway, this is still so, which is not strange. Vidkun Quisling was a Norwegian military officer. He was the founder of our National Socialist party in 1933. He visited Hitler in 1939. On 9 April 1940, the Germans invaded Norway. Vidkun Quisling declared himself Prime Minister that same day. He remained the leading collaborator until the German surrender in May 1945. He was arrested the day after, brought to court, defended by a highly regarded lawyer, but sentenced to death. An appeal to the Supreme Court was dismissed and he was executed on 24 October 1945.

His name became a synonym. But Quisling was not alone in collabo-
rating with the occupiers. Of a population of 3.5 million at that time,
80,000 became members of the Nazi party. And many more assisted the
occupiers – some as workers, others as informers or directly as torturers
in the service of the Gestapo. A special term was used: Collaborators
were called *landssvikere*. This meant something worse than just being
traitors. It meant deceiving the country, letting down the whole nation,
the major basis for identity and sovereignty during war and occupation.

7.7 The purge

The headlines on the very first newspaper that appeared in Norway the
day after German capitulation were: RO – ORDEN – VERDIGHET.
TRANQUILLITY, ORDER, DIGNITY, do not take private action, let
the state authorities administer the punishment which certainly and
justly will follow. And indeed, it followed. All members of the Nazi party,
even completely passive ones, were brought before the judicial authorities.
Particularly during the first years after the occupation the sentences were
severe in the extreme. More than 40,000 persons received some sort of
punishment, 17,000 in the form of imprisonment. Twenty-five Norwegians
were executed. Twelve Germans met the same destiny.

7.8 Preventing private vengeance

Quisling did not get away with it, nor did his followers. The thought of
meeting Quisling in the streets of Oslo some time after the end of the
German occupation was close to inconceivable as well as intolerable.
Some sort of peace was re-established by what happened to Quisling and
his collaborators.

This calmed the situation just after the German surrender. Private
vengeance was relatively rare, except for particularly cruel degradation
ceremonies carried out against women who had had relations with German
soldiers, and also grim actions taken against their children (Olsen 1998).
With these exceptions, a country of peace regained some of its peace.

But that was a peace with costs attached.

7.9 Narvik, October 2002

In October 2002, quite an extraordinary meeting took place in Narvik, a
city high up in the north of Norway. Narvik became famous in 1940 for
the extremely fierce fighting taking place there between German forces
on the one side, and British, French, Polish and Norwegian forces on

the other. A great number of soldiers died. They are buried in the grave-yard in the centre of Narvik. In 1942–3, new catastrophes occurred close to the town. A ship of misery arrived. It had Yugoslavian prisoners on board, prisoners deported to the far north as part of Hitler's programme of *Nacht und Nebel*. A camp was raised. After the first winter, only 30 per cent of the prisoners were still alive.

And then the meeting in 2002, 60 years after these occurrences. It was a meeting for peace and reconciliation. Here we were, representatives of all the involved nations. Some were war veterans, but also young soldiers from various nations attended, with ambassadors, the President of the Norwegian Parliament, the mayor of Narvik and also some academics. We met at the graveyard; German graves to the left, Allied graves lined up in front and to the right. We met in church with parts of prayers in all the languages represented. And we met at seminars on the theory and practice of reconciliation.

We were all there.

Or were we?

German war veterans had been invited and had accepted. But veterans are old now, and sick. The German ones did not appear. What a relief. Norwegian war veterans had grudgingly agreed to meet them. Now they were spared; only the German ambassador arrived.

But another category was not invited at all. The followers of Vidkun Quisling were not there. Not a single former collaborator could be seen. 'I could not have been here if they had been invited,' said the leading Norwegian war veteran, who was also a survivor of concentration camps in Germany. I know him as a kind and decent man. 'Well', he added, 'if they clearly had admitted their old wrongdoings, that would have been a different situation.' In the heated debate that followed, the chair-man exclaimed, directing his question to me: 'Would you accept a former torturer here, for reconciliation?'

I would.

7.10 The monument

We were also visiting the site of the old concentration camp just outside of Narvik. A monument was raised there. According to the text on the stone, this was 'a gift of gratitude from the Norwegian and Yugoslavian people in memory of the more than 500 Yugoslavs, victims of Nazism, who died in the German . . . camp 1942–43'.

Died? They were killed.

German camp? Yes, organized and directed by the German SS. But the guards were Norwegians, several hundred of them. After the war, 47 among them were brought before penal courts and given very severe prison sentences. I knew them well. As mentioned above, I had talked with most of them some time after the end of the occupation, and also with those guards who in the same camp had not behaved particularly badly. The court cases were thoroughly reported in the Norwegian media.

7.11 Delayed costs of punishment

What happened in Narvik last October is no evidence, but an illustration. The collaborators and war criminals were all severely punished after the occupation had come to an end. But the grand-scale punishments had not eradicated the hatred in the population. The collaborators are still despised in Norway, some of their children feel like outcasts, even grand-children keep quiet about their family history. A considerable segment of the population is thereby up to this day outside respectable society. And most Norwegians continue to think that killing in concentration camps was an activity reserved for Germans.

7.12 International penal courts and tribunals

The Nuremberg court was clearly a court established by the winners. It was international only in the sense that the four judges came from the four major countries that defeated Germany. And it was a court passing judgment on an enemy that had suffered total defeat. No wonder that Dresden, Hiroshima and Nagasaki, and the Gulags were not on the agenda.

In more recent attempts to establish international standards, this situation has to some extent changed. Some courts have gone more international. The International Criminal Tribunal for the former Yugoslavia in The Hague and the similar one for Rwanda situated in Arusha in Tanzania are examples. The new International Penal Court now established is intended to be of that type.

But it is clear that their international character is a highly limited one. This is most clear in respect of the International Penal Court. The most powerful among nations have not accepted to be under its authority. The USA has not ratified and has even put severe pressure on other nations to obtain their signed guarantees that they will not bring charges against US citizens before the International Penal Court. The Russian federation and Israel are other powerful nations who have not ratified the agreement. Those with power have a tendency to act in this way.

There are other problems with international courts. International politics is one. While I was first preparing some writing on this theme in spring 2001, Yugoslavian authorities were under enormous pressure to send Milosevic to the Tribunal in The Hague. If the government sent him to The Hague, they would receive money from the West to rebuild the country. If they only brought him to court at home, they would receive nothing. They sent him to The Hague.[2]

The International Tribunal for Rwanda illustrates other problems. The Tribunal is situated in Arusha in Tanzania. It costs annually millions of dollars to run. It is created for the élite suspects – some 100 people waiting for trial in a decent prison nearby. The idea behind it was that the major culprits ought to be sentenced first. But this means that the smaller fishes have to wait. They do that waiting in prisons across the border, in Rwanda. Some 120,000 prisoners have here been stored away under conditions bound to kill many more among them than the total number to be sentenced by the International Tribunal in Arusha. In 1999, 3,000 died in prisons in Rwanda.[3] Happily Rwanda, in the year 2002, started a system of Gacaca tribunals, a system based on lay people, and with a purpose closer to mediation and restoration.

*   *   *

I have no definite answers to the problems here raised. What I cannot hide is a deep ambivalence, bordering on scepticism, regarding international penal law as an answer to atrocities. Penal law always creates restrictions on the flow of information and is therefore not the best instrument to clarify what happened. International penal law is inevitably the law of the winners, and therefore of dubious utility in attempts to create social peace. It is an instrument to describe parts of what happened in the past. But we need systems that look forward. We need instruments that both clarify the past and help the future. Systems for truth and reconciliation might be one answer.

7.13 Truth commissions

Truth commissions represent systematic attempts to break silence, combined with trust in the strength of truth. Archbishop Tutu was central in creating an arena for exposure in South Africa. People forced into unbelievable degradation in the form of physical and mental pain were given an opportunity to tell their stories. They could do so eye-to-eye with their oppressors. And what is essential, independently of much criticism that has also hit the commissions, is that they were given the opportunity to concentrate on what they had seen, what they had experienced, and not on the matter of revenge, particularly not on the task of getting anybody formally sentenced. If it had been a penal court, the commission would have been forced to limit the flow of information to what was seen as legally relevant. And those telling their tales would have been met with doubts and cross-examinations from the other side.

Some of these were also essential elements in the situation of the oppressors. Mostly they appeared before the truth commission as an alternative to being brought into a penal court. When they talked, they talked under stress. And they had much to defend, such as self-respect and honour. But they had agreed to break the silence, to participate, to expose what they knew. And they could talk within a framework that was not determined by legal constraints.

Did they tell the truth?

If the point was to establish guilt for concrete acts according to the criteria of penal law, we cannot be sure. Perhaps more accurate information might have been revealed. Penal courts are exceptionally well-designed for that activity. But if the point is to allow for the totality of the occurrences, particularly as the parties saw it, then the truth commissions have considerable advantages. They open up an arena for exposure, for complaints, for emotional displays – and also for denials. If the central point is to expose what happened, not to decide on the delivery of pain, truth commissions have a considerable advantage.[4]

For the purpose of *preventing errors* in the delivery of pain, the penal law arrangements – when they are functioning properly and sometimes they are not – are probably the best that can be invented. But when it comes to a more thorough exposure of what happened, followed by a potential for the healing of wounds, truth commissions – if they are functioning properly and sometimes they are not – are probably better instruments than penal courts. One reservation: This is an ideal-typical picture. Several truth commissions have worked under highly unfavourable conditions, politically and/or economically. They have thereby experienced trouble, as penal courts in the same situation would also have experienced.

7.14 Reconciliation

Truth is one important step. But to create peace, more steps must be taken. Most important: there is also a need for reconciliation.

That process has two parts. First, there is the question of *compensation* for the victims. It is fine that truth is established; it becomes clear what has happened in the past when what are often rich and powerful offenders meet very poor victims. But truth and excuses are not enough. The basic problem of inequality remains after some common understanding of history has been established. These problems must also be approached, but are often ignored in these processes. The affluent offender goes home to his comfortable villa after having told the truth, while the former prisoner goes back to material misery.

The second question has to do with *mediation*, leading towards peace-making. The question can be raised as to whether peace is at all possible after years of oppression, years of killings and rape, maybe also serious attempts at genocide. Of course, it is not possible, completely. Husbands are killed, those raped are left with their scars and maybe also with children intentionally forced on them by the enemy. Or they are, as were travellers in my country, a gypsy-related group, brought into a situation where they are sterilized, or their children are taken to unknown addresses by the authorities. These evil acts can never be undone.

Particularly complicated in Europe during recent years has been the situation in Kosovo, with its highly deplorable Serbian acts, with highly deplorable Western interference, and also with highly deplorable Kosovo-Albanian acts. Before the bombing, there were 1,300 international peace observers in Kosovo. They were withdrawn so that the bombing might commence. Most observers seem to agree that 13,000 international peace observers could have kept peace in Kosovo, and thus prevented bombings and the flight of 800,000 civilians. Recently, there were 45,000 foreign soldiers in the province.

There are two ways to address the Kosovo conflict. There is the usual penal one: kill the killers, imprison them or harm them in other ways. Or one could help conflicting parties to meet, create an arena where they can tell their stories, expose their grievances, and then slowly, maybe after many, many attempts, come to some sort of common understanding of what happened and what might be done to alleviate the situation.

The utmost naivety?

Not quite. A very strong influence on modern penal policy these days stems from the native traditions in New Zealand, Australia, and from the native Indian culture, particularly in Canada, but also in the USA. It has become clear how heavily native youngsters are overrepresented in modern prisons. Thereby the need for returning to the old ways of coping with conflicts has been exposed. These old ways are based on mediation. In relatively egalitarian societies far away from the central authorities, it is close to obvious that punishment might lead to civil war, just as punishments in the international arena without one central power can lead to the renewal of old conflicts and warfare. In such societies, it becomes essential to restore the situation and thereby preserve social systems. Restore is an Old Norse term. It means, literally, to raise once more those wooden stocks – *staur* – that have fallen down, or more relevantly here, to rebuild the house. These activities represent a negation of the ideals of penal law. If blame and shame is to be applied, it has to be in the form of reintegrative shaming. If an offender is clearly defined, emphasis is put on how he or she can repair the damage, materially or symbolically, and not on how that person can be brought to suffer. Restorative meetings of this type are in many ways a further development of truth commissions.

Not possible in the Balkan region?

I encountered that statement in Tirana, the capital of Albania, some years ago. It was at a huge meeting with hundreds of participants. The theme was how to end blood vengeance. 'Impossible', said several of the participants. 'We are proud, so the rules of blood vengeance have to be obeyed.' Then rose a huge, white-haired man. I later learned he had served as a general with the guerrilla forces against the Italian occupiers and later in the army. But that was a long time ago. Now he said: 'I have been imprisoned for so many years under Hoxa [the former ruler of Albania]. Now it is over. I feel no hatred. Albanians are not that way, they are not a peculiar sort.' The discussion immediately came to an end. The project on mediation is by now well established in Albania.

But reconciliation is at least not possible when monsters are behind the atrocities!

As mentioned before, I have worked with crime and punishment most of my life, but never met a monster. I could not find them among killers in concentration camps, nor have I met any since then. There are people I dislike, but none that are completely impossible to reach, at least for some important moments. My supposition is that we all, as humans, have had some common experiences. We are all nursed during the early stage of our life, and most of us have also later had some common experiences, positive or negative. A minimum of common ground is thereby created, a platform where we are able to recognize bits of similarities to other humans.

It might also prove possible to expand such a platform. We might come across a person who despises gypsies and systematically attempts to harm them. Nonetheless, we might be able to find a platform of agreement on caring for relatives. Slowly, it might prove possible to see gypsies as a population who ranked extraordinarily high on care for those close to them, and therefore a population that has to be included in the category of those not to be harmed.

But even with genuine communication, even in a situation where we have been able to see each other as common human beings, we might be forced to use force.[5] There might be dark corners of my soul I am unable to control, even if I am aware of danger. It might have been correct to use force against me to prevent unacceptable behaviour.

Situations might occur where imprisonment is the last resort. So also in political conflicts. I might have much in common with a person who stubbornly fights for goals I find unacceptable. I might be brought to a point where I saw no other solution than counterforce.

What then is the point of insisting that we have some common ground with all people and that it is possible and important to find some fellow human traits everywhere?

Because this is essential for the control of the controller. The perception of the other person as a monster, one completely outside normal humanity, makes it possible to ignore basic rules for how to relate to other people as fellow human beings. The idea that monsters exist is dangerous for all, but particularly dangerous for those among us with the formal task of controlling other people's behaviour.

But when the acts are completely out of the acceptable, unbelievable. Genocide?

Many nations are based on genocide, my own included. To the best of our ability, Norwegians made attempts to exterminate the Sami people, our indigenous population, and particularly its culture. I have met Sami people who were physically punished if they talked their own language in school. But in the 1990s the remaining Samis got their own parliament. It was in compensation for a particularly ugly destruction of one of their major salmon rivers. Quite recently the University of Oslo, which is my university, also gave back to the Sami a whole collection of skulls. These had been gathered for study purposes by physical anthropologists and exhibited for years not far away from an office I had for a period. I did not reflect on it, at that time. Several of these Samis had been executed for sorcery, some for opposition to Norwegian authorities. I admit that these sins are old and small compared to the white man's behaviour in Africa or America. But not small for the Sami population, confronting what they might have seen as Norwegian monsters.

What I am trying to convey is that atrocities are general features of human history, parts of our destiny. Many nations have been involved, as victims or as perpetrators, often as both. It is important to include atrocities in the normality of abnormality. We must find ways of both preventing and reacting to atrocities where we mobilize the common stock of knowledge on how to handle social conflicts.

But if the acts are fully, completely out of the usual? As the acts initiated by Osama bin Laden as they are seen from a Western perspective, or with acts initiated by Ariel Sharon as they are seen from a Palestinian point of view? Can they be seen in a peace creating framework? Am I willing to negotiate with the Devil, in Hell or with those seen as his brothers?

Again, I am.

What happened on 11 September was deeply repulsive, directed as the action was at non-military victims. Difficult to understand, but not impossible. Atrocities, but not carried out by monsters. Distant from the ordinary, but not so distant that dialogue is completely out of the question. In short, a case where tools from social sciences in general and criminology and peace research in particular might be applicable.

We must always try to initiate negotiations. Before and preferably instead of violence and at any point later on, attempts must be made to create conditions for dialogue. We ought to meet those we think have done something terribly wrong; we must attempt to understand why they have done it, attempt to present alternative ways for perceiving the acts and also look for some common ground. How can we otherwise stop violence if we let opposing parties dig down in their separate and divided understandings of their situation? Seen from the perspective of preventing violence, the US is probably more protected by conversations than by bombs.

Maybe nothing will come out of such conversations. But it would be ethically valid and may be also useful to make attempts to try to get to know how the parties perceive matters before weapons are admitted. Maybe, maybe, it might be possible that parties, little by little, would come to see that the other side also had a point.

7.15 The importance of not having answers

My major conclusion from attempts to find answers to atrocities is that there are no easy answers in individual cases, and maybe no good answers in general. This sounds negative, and it is intended so. Pretensions of having answers might be counterproductive. There are many vested interests behind the claims of having the right answers. So much is launched as answers to atrocities, which actually increase the chances for further atrocities. Penal action might strengthen certain nations, or forces within those nations, but weaken others. It might also carry the seeds of new atrocities. International courts, deviating so much from the ordinary ideals of the courts, might prevent a deeper understanding of the forces behind mass-scale killings. A conclusion that there are no good answers to atrocities is not a heroic one; it is not one that will initiate strong actions, or immediately create new defences against evil forces. But maybe by admitting to the non-existence of good answers we create a foundation on which to build peace. If the hunt for good answers is a vain one, we are forced back to the ordinary civil ways of handling conflicts; talks, mediation, restoration – and civil and penal courts where that can prevent escalation.

We have to live with sorrow and misery in the shadow of atrocities. But we must at the same time also try out some old-fashioned ways of solving conflict, maybe even before the culprits have moved so far as to ask for this. We do not want amnesia. But, after all the information has been brought to the surface, imprinted in all our minds and all human history, we might in the end have no better final solution than forgiveness and restoration.

8   When is enough, enough?

With a perspective on crime as an endless natural resource, we can raise some questions which are rarely made explicit. We can ask: When is enough, enough, or, eventually, when is it too little crime? What are the suitable types and volumes of acts seen as crime? And following that, what is the suitable amount of control through the penal apparatus – eventually, what is the suitable number of officially stigmatized sinners? How large can we let the penal system grow, or conversely, how small can we have it, if we need it at all? Is it possible to establish upper, and eventually lower, limits to the amount of punishment that ought to be applied in a modern society? And lastly, for those of us working close to this field, is it possible to influence what happens?

8.1   Penal systems as signs

Penal systems carry deep meanings. They convey information on central features of the states they represent. Nothing told more about Nazi Germany, about the USSR or about Maoist China than their penal apparatus – from their police practice, via courts to prisons, camps and Gulags. In concrete cases, we can evaluate states according to their penal systems. We are, by our standards and values, our likes and dislikes, able to say that there is something wrong within that particular state. Or we might like what we see, and evaluate the state accordingly.

Such an evaluation might be related to four major features:

1   *The types of crimes reacted against* within a state. Certain regimes might simply be seen to punish acts that citizens in other states feel ought not to have been punished (e.g. political or religious opposition).
2   *The forms of decision making* used when questions of delivery of pain are to be considered. States might be seen as employing unacceptable methods such as confessions after torture or measures close to torture.

Or they might operate without a jury, without an independent defence, behind closed doors, or with judges who are politically biased or not free by belonging to special categories such as priests, freemasons or military officers.

3   The question of *the nature of the receivers* of the intended pain, particularly how representative they are of the population in general with regard to age, gender, race, class, etc. An extremely biased prison population might indicate severe defects somewhere in that system.

4   The question of *the volume and forms of punishment.* Extremely high volumes and particularly painful forms might indicate certain deplorable peculiarities in the use of intended pain within the system.

It is this last point, and particularly the question of volume, that will stay in the centre of my discussion in what now follows.[1]

My question here is one close to the title of this book: A *suitable amount of crime.* We have seen that social organization determines what is seen as crime. Then the next question follows: Is it possible to establish *some sort of criteria* for what might be seen as the suitable amount of punishment in a society? And in this connection, is it possible to say that one state is better than another state when it comes to the volume of punishment? And particularly, is it possible to say that a state with a small volume of punishment is a better state than one with a large volume?

Intuitively, we might feel it easy to do so. Or we can find cases so far out that any reasoning seems superfluous. Hitler's concentration camps are in a way outside of what can be discussed, constructed for working to death or for direct extermination. The Soviet situation until long after World War II was also obviously beyond all standards, both in the volume of prisoners and in living conditions.

But turned into questions of the evaluation of the volume and of the life conditions of prisoners in modern times, when is here enough, enough? And when is it more than enough? Where is the limit in modern societies? When has a prison population in a country reached a level when at least our intuition says that this is wrong, completely wrong, unacceptable! And when are life conditions below dignity? We have some intuitive answers. The reader will hopefully at this point in the book know where my heart is on these matters. But is it possible to anchor views from the heart to some sort of reasoning?

*   *   *

Let me attempt to do so by the discussion of three cases of IF.

1. *IF we believe in the values of kindness and forgiving*
– then we ought to keep the institution of penal law a small one.

As human beings, we have, most of us, internalized some basic concerns as to what we can and cannot do to other people. To express it in the spirit of Cooley (1902): Without being met with a minimum of kindness and care, we can never grow up, never develop into human beings. Basic are such rules as:

Be kind
Do not kill
Do not use torture
Do not intentionally inflict harm
Forgiveness ranks above retribution

These are core values. Without entering into any deep discussion of natural law, I dare to say that these values are in a way above discussion – they are obvious. And it is equally obvious that punishment represents a break with these values. It is as if we often forget what punishment is all about; that it is an act with the intention of causing other humans to suffer. Punishment means delivery of pain intended as pain. Punishment is an activity in basic disharmony with these other cherished values. An eye for an eye was a restrictive command; not a demand. Punishment is used everywhere, accepted everywhere, but nonetheless, the activity stands in conflict with other central values.

Delivery of pain is the core element of punishment, even in countries without torture or the death penalty. With imprisonment, we do not take the whole life away. But we take parts of life away. With life-long imprisonment, we take close to all life away. Or as Zigmunt Bauman (2000, p. 209) sees the Maxi-Maxi prisons with their total isolation of prisoners: 'Apart from the fact that the prisoners are still eating and defecating, their cells could be mistaken for coffins.'

Delivery of pain is an activity in basic disharmony with other cherished values. From an ethical point of view, a society with a small amount of pain infliction is therefore preferable to one with a large amount. Torture and death were once seen as obvious forms of punishment. Today, they are out in most countries close to our culture. The non-existence of torture and capital punishment can be seen as the Crown Jewels *in absentia* of our penal system. Their absence is our pride. But imprisonment also comes close to taking life away. It means to take *most* of what is usually included in life away. Incarceration has not gained the same protection against use as torture and capital punishment.

To me, a small prison population within a state has some of the same sacred qualities as the absence of torture and capital punishment. Its absence makes some of the disharmony in our system less pronounced.

It gives thereby more space to life according to our most sacred values. When these values are threatened, we must change the *conditions* threatening them. Not the values.

So, if we believe in values of kindness and forgiving, we ought to keep the institution of penal law, with its intentional use of pain intended as pain, at the lowest possible level.

2. IF *we believe in the values of keeping civil societies civil*
– then we have to keep the institution of penal law a small one.

It is, of course, perfectly possible to control a large amount of unwanted behaviour through police actions followed by punishments. I know, having grown up during a military occupation. A Norwegian flag on the collar might mean imprisonment. When that flag was seen as too dangerous, a paper clip might do – they keeps things together, as a population in opposition. But the occupiers understood it, the clips were banned some carriers of clips arrested, and the use of this symbol in public places diminished. Or in modern times: To drive without a safety belt is dangerous. A few well-publicized heavy fines bring that dangerous habit to a minimum. Motor bikers have to use a helmet. Disobedience is very easy to control – no great burden for the penal apparatus.

Punishment is a heavy tool. Citizens are to receive pain. Such a purpose demands power. Within our cultures, this means building up strict forms of control of the use of power and intended pain. While civil life contains a mixture of formal and informal interaction, the penal institution will be dominated by formality – to protect those who might receive pain, but also those that deliver pain.

Interaction between free citizens is the prototype of civil life. Much of it can be exemplified by life in primary relationships. Civility implies here to meet at a personal level, as full persons, not in strictly regulated and deliminated roles. Also primary control can be strong and abusive. But in relatively open and, to some extent, egalitarian relations, control will be partly based on mutuality. Control is built into the relationship. This might also lead to abuse where formal action becomes inevitable; the violent partner is a core example. The problem is only how often state intervention also fails, and how often it gets the alternatives to disintegrate, alternatives such as crisis centres, joint female actions or neighbours' intervention. 'Also this Saturday night she screamed badly. Why don't the police interfere?'

3. IF *we believe in the value of living in cohesive, integrated societies*
– then we must retard the growth of the institution of penal law.

A strong growth of penal institutions represents a serious threat to ideals of social cohesion and assimilation. As long as those seen as extremely deviant or basically criminal in their behaviour are few and far between, prosecution and punishment might increase cohesion in society in general. With a small prison population, it is possible to think of deviance as an *exception*. It is accepted wisdom among us that normality is only strengthened by the awareness of some rare cases of abnormality. But with a large prison population, the metaphor moves from deviance to war. The cohesive society with some helpful outsiders is transformed into the divided one with large segments seen as potentially dangerous for the social order of that totality. At the same time, for those hit by punishment, prisons are converted from places of shame to more ordinary parts of social life.

A huge prison population also means a great drain of young males from inner cities, particularly from minority groups there. Thwarted are the possibilities for normal development, the creation of families and the care for children, for education and paid labour. Young females living in the inner cities sometimes compare their life situation with war conditions. There are so few males around, so few possibilities to establish some form of family life. And if established, the chances are great that it will be dissolved because the man disappears into prison. Some would perhaps welcome this effect, but ought at the same time to be made aware that here are created conditions far away from those usually found within democratic societies.

The alternative to war conditions and mass incarceration is of course to give these populations an ordinary share of ordinary society – education, work, and political and cultural participation. The present use of mass imprisonment blocks the way for such developments.

Mr Halvdan Koht, former Minister of Foreign Affairs for Norway and professor of history, once stated it this way:[2]

> The building of our nation has been a long process in which class patriotism has been transformed into national patriotism . . . each time a new class arose, and demanded its rights and power in society, it seemed as if hatred emerged and that the seed was planted that could destroy society as a whole. Eventually, however, when the lower classes achieved their goals, it appeared that society had added to itself new dimensions and become much richer than before.

8.2 The lower limit

There are solid reasons behind attempts to counteract the present expansion of the penal institutions. In a global situation where the pressures all the time are for an expansion of penal law, and an expansion of prison populations, it is clear that the general advice must be opposition to this development. Let us decrease the condition creating unacceptable behaviour, let us limit the size of the penal apparatus, and particularly, let us do our utmost to reduce the volume of pain delivery. A suitable amount can in this situation only be found if we move in the opposite direction to the present one.

But this view must not be carried into the absurd. There are, even in the best of societies, situations where generally accepted values are threatened. There are situations where those that threaten them are unwilling to refrain from their attempts, or not willing to meet those they might have damaged in a process of reconciliation, or where those damaged are not willing to meet them. For those situations and people, we have the institution of penal law as a treasure in society.

There is one particular danger in a total shrinkage of the penal system: If the need is there, strongly felt, penal measures might be introduced under false labels. Power will be used, but without the measures of control developed within penal law described in the foregoing. Another danger is to hide delivery of pain behind a mantle of treatment. The USSR had their mental institutions for dissidents. As mentioned in my preface, 'Roots', Norway had once what we called compulsory treatment for alcohol problems. It was a special measure for those so poor that they had to consume their liquor in public places, exposing their misery to everybody. The treatment took place in a particularly severe prison where they were kept for years. It would have been a case of grave injustice to have them there as punishment, said one of the experts. But as treatment, no objections could be raised. I fear that one of the these days so popular 'drug courts' – they are supposed to be more lenient than the ordinary penal courts – might contain some of the same dangers as our old special measures against the skid row population.

So, there is a minimum, a lower limit for the reduction of the institution of penal law. But to warn against a transgression of that limit is a warning of the same type as the old one against flooding in the Sahara. Our attention must be turned to the other side, the danger of the abnormal punitive society.

8.3 Is defeat inevitable?

An essential question for us in the Nordic countries, and also in Western Europe and Canada, is whether the developments in the US are inevitable. Are they a consequence of their economic system? And will welfare states also gradually face consequences similar to the US model, consequences that will lead to increased class differentiation as well as to increased uncertainty among the population at large? We observe how the criminal policies of a number of industrial nations are becoming a central arena for presentation by politicians. Without control of the international economy, the need for being in control of the consequences of the deregulated economy becomes pressing. Uncertainties, frequent changes, and degrading life circumstances for the most vulnerable segments of the population characterize the deregulated employment market. Uncertainties are muffled by political promises about severe measures to be taken against *offenders*, a term that gradually has become a euphemism for *the lower-lower classes*, a term that may become a euphemism for *the dangerous classes* or in certain countries people of the wrong colour. With these transformations, the situation is ripe for war-like conditions. 'You helped us win the war against our external enemy,' a former US Minister of Justice exclaimed to a group of military experts. And she continued: 'Now you must help us win the war against criminality at home.' The result of that war is found in the prison population of more than two million inhabitants.

Will those of us not yet there be able to resist a similar development?

I am far from convinced that we will succeed. But the matter is so important that it here is right to use some old-fashioned terms: We have a moral obligation to do our utmost to hinder such a development. As researchers in this field, we are in great danger of becoming the willing executors of this development if we keep quiet. Criminologists in particular stand so close to punishment that we have exceptional responsibilities as whistle blowers.

In a way, we are in a parallel situation to several of our colleagues in the natural sciences. They observe the damaging effects, locally or globally, of industrial development and of our way of organizing life: the new factories, more burning of oil, more cars, more planes, more contaminated air and water, and a creeping warming up of the whole globe. It is bound to create serious damage. They cry out, many do, against these threats.

We are in exactly the same situation! We observe the creeping damage done to our social systems. And we have to act in the same manner as responsible natural scientists are doing. As Patricia Rawlinson formulated this point in a recent conversation on these parallels: Criminologists must become the Greenpeace for social systems!

In this situation, we have to tell about crime as a social construction. We have to go into the phenomena of unwanted behaviour, describe the many ways of looking at it, and the consequences of the various perceptions. We have to reveal the general forces leading both to the unwanted behaviour as well as to the perception of these acts. And we have to mobilize our sociological imagination in attempts to give advice on alternatives.

Much is already said in the foregoing chapters, here therefore only a general point: We should not always start with offences and offenders, and then ask what ought to be done. We should turn the whole thing upside down. We should start with the system of sanctions and here take basic values as our point of departure. We should ask: What sort of pain and what sort of distribution of pain do we find acceptable for our type of society? How large can we accept the penal sector of society to grow without endangering values of kindness, the civil character of our society and the cohesive character of that society? And then, when these limits are established, and we observe that they are threatened or transgressed, we have to give advice on what ought to be done. The level of punishment must be elevated to that of the independent variable. Conditions creating unwanted behaviour and followed by demand for punishment should be degraded to becoming the dependent ones, those to be changed. We cannot say, not concretely and exactly, when enough is enough. But we can say that punishment is an activity low in the rank of values. Punishment should therefore be the last alternative, not the first one. We could say, and ought to say, that these costs must be introduced in the planning procedures. Economic gains must here be seen in relation to penal costs.

8.4 Reintegrative shaming of national states?

But does it matter what we say? Are we as professionals within the field of deviance and control at all able to influence the development we can see unfolding these days and years? Not much, but let me describe some personal experiences, and also some road blocks ahead. I will depart from the term that so much of the writing of John Braithwaite[3] circles around: reintegrative shaming. It is a concept from the core activity in deviance control: Your acts were deplorable, bad, wrong. We have to tell you. Shame to you. But otherwise you are OK. Stop acting wrongly, come home and we will slaughter the lamb, have a big meal and celebrate your homecoming. To reintegrate the person, both the negative and the positive must be exposed. It is in this respect that punishment is such an inefficient tool. In a reintegrative perspective, a prisoner released after serving should always be met with an orchestra outside the walls. Later should follow the big, integrative feast. That would have been reintegration.

Then to shame at the state level:

Observing countries is like reading books. As a criminologist, I am also a cultural worker. As cultural workers, criminologists could function as book reviewers. We must describe what we observe or read and evaluate it according to explicit standards. And we have to attempt to inform about our observations.

Often it is not necessary to do more. Important decision makers will see themselves with the eyes of the observer and initiate changes in their penal policy.

This was what happened in Finland, far back in the 1960s. I had made a study comparing prison figures in Denmark, Finland, Norway and Sweden and was giving a lecture on some of the results at the Faculty of Law in Helsinki. A major finding was that Finland was completely out of line compared to figures from the other Nordic countries. It was a reminder to us that the country once had been a Russian province, and still was similar to Russia in certain respects I had no intention to change anything through this lecture, just to explain. I was young and modest at that time. But the figures created a shock in the audience and triggered several modifications in their system. Finland wanted, culturally, to be a part of Scandinavia, not of Russia. That was particularly important in Stalinist times just after World War II.

*   *   *

Russia today is a country out of line with Europe, also when it comes to the number of prisoners. But important parts of their intelligentsia want the country to be part of Western Europe. Visitors are invited to observe and to reveal their observations. Penal Reform International[4] is one of the most active participants in this process. I am only a very small part in all this.

As a visitor to Russia, I get some of the feeling of visiting Finland in the old days, in meeting a culture where it is uncomfortable to experience oneself as in too great a distance to common European standards. This is also the case when it comes to the question of the relative size of the prison population. It is with considerable embarrassment, from the very top and down, that the Russians reveal the total size of their prison population and also the conditions in their remand prisons. My own theme while lecturing at universities or colleges in Russia is to emphasize the urgent need for reduction of the number of prisoners. There is, I say, no point in talks about psychological treatment or education in a system so desperately overcrowded as the Russian one. The rewards for the police must be related to clearing the case, not to getting the culprit in a cell. If Russia wants to be an ordinary part of Europe, it must also be so when it comes to prison population.

Estonia, Latvia and Lithuania are in the same situation. They want to come close to Scandinavia; there is just some water that divides us, and much in the culture is similar. But the proximity builds on an illusion if they preserve a penal apparatus belonging to another time and another culture. Can the general culture in a country remain uninfluenced by this? One might also expect that countries with such huge numbers of prisoners would create perfect growth conditions for anti-social sub-cultures. People trained in these types of subcultures will not be the most welcome ambassadors for their countries when they visit the Scandinavia they are supposed to stand so close to.

The embarrassment among many officials in these countries has another side: It is today with considerable pride that some of them report on the *reduction* of their prison population, particularly in their remand prisons. This development is a manifestation of Russia coming closer to Europe. In this reduction, we get at the same time an illustration of a major issue in this book: Prison figures are not shaped by crime, but by the general culture. Another change is also reported with pride among some: Russia has, by now, abolished capital punishment. That was necessary to get admitted to the Council of Europe.

But these reductions are far from stabilized. Two wars threaten. First, the war in Chechenya and all the violence directly and indirectly connected to this. The second threat is the war against drugs. Penal reformers are not the only visitors to Russia. Drug experts are there also. I have spent depressing hours in the Duma, listening to a parliamentarian with much power who described the importance of protecting the Russian youth against drugs. It will develop into an epidemic, he said. One user drags ten newcomers into the habit, and so it will continue. Severe punishment becomes a necessity to stop this epidemic spreading. I had heard it before. The lost war against drugs in the West is now dangerously close to being repeated in the East, with predictable results.

The situation south of the Russian border gives little hope for reduction of prison populations there: Belarus does not change. It is simply a totalitarian system. They do not want to be part of Western Europe. They want to be as Russia was, and also to influence Russia to be what it was. I think that explains their increase in prison numbers and also their anger as when the woman judge I told of in Chapter 4 would no longer participate. And of course they have not abolished capital punishment. I was brought down to the basement of one of their major prisons. Here were two prisoners awaiting for execution in a narrow cell. I was able to turn down an offer to look at them through the peephole and focused my attention on the sneering dogs at the end of the corridor. Just months before, two other prisoners awaiting execution had committed suicide in the same cell. They hanged themselves, together, with the same rope.

Nonetheless, the situation in Russia, the greatest incarcerator in Europe, is not without hope. The increase in the number of prisoners has come to a stop and a slight reduction can be observed. There exists a willingness to discuss the problems and the atmosphere makes an open discussion of these matters possible.

* * *

Just weeks before the manuscript for this book went to the publisher, I spent some days lecturing in Cuba. Usually, I get to know a country through its penal system, but that was not particularly easy in this case. I did not get access to any of their prisons. And their prison figures are state secrets, just as in the Soviet Union back in time. But of course, the USSR figures were not impossible to estimate. I have described the basis for my estimates in *Crime Control as Industry* (Christie 2000). When it comes to the Cuban situation, there are miserable holes in my knowledge. I can offer only rough estimates. For example, against prostitutes Cuba applies measures they do not call punishment. I do not know for how many and under what sort of conditions they live there.

But I feel pretty sure that Cuba belongs to the category of countries with a very high rate of incarceration. My estimate is that they now, in 2003, probably have somewhere between 50,000 and 60,000 prisoners; my guess is that they are closer to the second figure than to the first. This means they have between 454 and 545 prisoners per 100,000 inhabitants. These are large numbers in a Caribbean connection. The figures also represent a great increase since 1997, when Cuba according to my estimate had less than 300 prisoners per 100,000 inhabitants. In 1987, their prison population was even smaller. Probably their prison figures have tripled since then. Cuba also has, this spring, executed three prisoners. For many years they have had a moratorium on capital punishment.

What is behind this development?

Cuba is a country under immense pressure from their large neighbour to the north. Their declared socialism combined with their stubborn nationalism leads to severe sanctions from the US. In addition, their economy was badly hurt when the USSR dissolved. To manage, they have to some extent opened their economy. United States dollars are now legitimate money in the country. Relatives from abroad send money to some. These become relatively affluent according to Cuban standards. Money from tourism is also difficult to control. All this makes it impossible to prevent both an extensive black market and increased internal differences. Haddad (2003) gives a detailed description of this whole situation. Life is difficult, and feels even more so since the difficulties are not experienced by all. Compared to most states close to it, Cuba has a highly developed welfare system for the most vulnerable part of the population. No illiteracy, no children that sleep in the streets. And they have a hospital system so well developed that the most conservative among Norwegian parliamentarians come home after visits and tell that we have much to learn from Cuba. Nonetheless, external pressure and internal differentiation take their toll. A vulnerable state bites, and a frustrated population tolerates these bites.

In addition comes the rigidity created by secrecy. The situation is in a way similar to the one in Finland after World War II. The Finns were not aware of how their large prison population deviated from the usual standards in Scandinavia, but changed when they became aware of it. With prison figures a state secret as they are in Cuba, it is not easy to initiate any discussion there on these matters. Secrecy also makes difficult any criticism of the inner working of the system. How are the judges selected, who are they, and what becomes their destiny if they deviate from the stern policy? Who are the prosecutors, how are they trained? And how are the prison guards selected and trained – and what are their values?

One last point on Cuba has to do with history and cultural tradition. The country feels as in war, and its history has also been an extremely bloody one. Here also the country on one important point has had the same historical experience as Russia and the USA: Cuba was a slave state. Not until 1868 was slavery totally abolished. Six years earlier they had close to half a million black slaves in a population of 1.4 million.

How to approach this problem? My attempt was the old one, to compare ideals with practice.

Cuba has *ideals* of creating an egalitarian society. It has ideals close to those in Scandinavian welfare states. There is a tradition of close contact between trade unions in Cuba and Scandinavia. But what happens with these ideals, when a state acquires an exceptionally large prison population?

I was not invited into any Cuban prison. But based on observation from large prisons in countries with some similarities to Cuba, I could at least suggest how such prisons usually develop: With that large number of prisoners, and with a system growing so quickly, prisons will obviously be large and overpopulated. They will have relatively few prison guards. This means that the prisoners themselves will rule the inner life of the prisons. This will lead to the development of a hierarchical system among the inmates. At the top will be a king, surrounded by his court. At his service will stand a group of thugs, controlling prisoners of lower ranks. Then there will be a great number of prisoners of more ordinary rank. And at the bottom will be the untouchables, those relegated to menial tasks, eventually functioning as prostitutes for the better-off among the prisoners. A caste system is created inside such systems. A system in extreme contrast to what Cuba strives to create for the society as a whole. I never asked if this picture was valid for Cuba, but I heard nothing to the contrary.

Here we are back to the question of the suitable amount of prisoners. What happens in a country with such a large prison population is that they here create an anti-society. They create a society that stands in extreme contrast to their dominant ideals. To preserve an egalitarian welfare state, they develop systems that are negations of welfare states. They create systems where the participants are efficiently trained for a life in direct contradiction to the ideals that the authorities in Cuba strive to attain. It cannot in the long run be useful. It will become a danger to the fundamental values of that society.

What I here have described is at the core of my attempts to shame some states to change penal policies. In addition, I have one other theme, when lecturing in Cuba and in other countries that deviate with their extremely large prison populations. That is on forms of alternative conflict solutions.

Often, huge prison populations are a recent development. In many countries, there were other solutions that earlier dominated – some of them rather Draconian, but some very peaceful. Here then, come references to alternative forms of conflict solutions: restorative justice and much of the material described in Chapters 6 and 7 of this book. This is not any imperialistic manoeuvre to force states into foreign measures. It is an attempt to connect states to their own roots, to document that a large prison population is not a destiny. Alternatives exist.

*　*　*

But I come from Norway, a small nation with considerable freedom of expression, with several political parties, with freedom to join whatever I want, with no restrictions on travel – at least if you are a Norwegian. With this background, am I not then obliged to confront Cuba with their limitations on these same freedoms? Particularly, would it not be right first and foremost to scold them for their imprisonment of political opponents?

My preference is to start at the other end, with ordinary prisoners. Imprisonment of political opponents is part of a political culture. That political culture is connected to the penal culture. States with large prison populations are in the habit of using that measure. The barriers against using imprisonment for political opponents are less solid in such states. The barrier against using capital punishment for political opponents is likewise less solid in countries where that measure is used extensively against what are seen as 'ordinary criminals'.

So also with torture. Once I was invited to the opening of a centre against torture in Greece. It was shortly after the fall of the military junta that after a coup had ruled the country. A statement from a former political prisoner is what I remember best: Had he been tortured? No, he said solemnly. But it had been awful to stay in that prison because of the cries from the ordinary prisoners under torture. Torture was a regular part of police methods. How could they otherwise clear up cases of crime in Greece? I later heard that one of their more important police chiefs had threatened to resign if he was denied access to this tool for efficient police work. He was denied it. I do not know if he resigned.

My point is simply that the best way to reduce the use of imprisonment for political opponents is to minimize the use of imprisonment in general. Most prisoners from all countries, independently of political systems, are poor and miserable. By improving their conditions, particularly by getting them out of prisons, we at the same time prevent the use of imprisonment against political opponents. Minimize prison populations, humanize prison conditions, abolish any use of capital punishment and torture, these are within our particular fields the best measures to protect political, as well as ethnic and socially deprived minority groups. I respect that some might be of the opinion that I ought to talk loudly and confront the one-party states with all their deviations from human rights in general and Norwegian standards in particular. But I will not. That is to start at the wrong end.

8.5 USA – the world champion

I do not feel at ease with what now follows. The USA – so close culturally, intellectually, emotionally. I have been there on several occasions and have always been received with warm hospitality. I am fond of many aspects of the country. In earlier days, I thought that if I could not live in Oslo, then I would choose New York City.

* * *

Compared to the old USSR and now Cuba, the USA is like an open book. Prison figures are easily available and clearly presented. There were big headlines in the US newspapers when their prison figures in June 2002 passed the two million mark and also in 2003 when one hundred thousand more were added. Perhaps that openness reflects some of the problem?

Basically, it seems as if their enormous prison population is *not* a source of shame. It is seen as a sort of inevitable answer to crime, if anything, a sign of strength and efficiency. Thre exists of course opposition to the dominant line, but this opposition can at least not be called strong or influential.

To me, the US penal system is a system that negates the fundamental values they claim as their own. It is an open society. Nobody censures my speech. I can move freely. I am even invited back. But what goes on in the US penal system for two million people, and for the additional more than four and a half million on probation and parole, has since long passed the level of what can be understood as reflecting their values. It is materially the wealthiest country in the world. Nonetheless, it is a country that uses prisons instead of welfare. It is a country that continuously talks about freedom. Nonetheless, it has the largest prison population in the world. It is a country that fought a fierce civil war in which the abolition of slavery was at least some of the motivation. Nonetheless, it has an abnormal proportion of black people within its prison walls. It is a country with great emphasis on sociability. Nonetheless, an exceptional number of their prisoners live under conditions of such a total isolation that nothing compares (King 1999). It is a country that emphasizes limits to state power. Nonetheless, it has an enormous number of employees to keep that state power at a maximum, both at a federal and state level. In sum, it is a country that uses exclusion instead of inclusion, and in addition executes a portion of the most unwanted.

United States penal policy represents a threat against human values in their own country. And also, out of concern for preserving the civil character of their own society, such an enormous penal sector represents a serious danger. But also abroad this penal policy is a danger, through its model power. Parliamentarians from my country go to New York to learn about zero tolerance. They are not alone in going. The danger is that it is we, the critical ones, who will be shamed into conformity with US standards.

*   *   *

How to behave in this situation? Should one, with some knowledge of prison matters, keep away from professional visits to a nation with this extensive penal apparatus? This is not my opinion. Such a position would be in total contrast to all I attempt to convey in this book. Of course, we should never cut off contact with those with whom we disagree.

On the contrary, we should go more often. But an absolute condition for professional visits to an open society such as the US must be a clear exposure of disagreement with their penal policy. It is necessary to expose that, seen from abroad, it is difficult to understand that the abnormal size of the US penal system does not become the completely dominant theme for colleagues in the US. It is difficult to understand why the very existence of this system does not become the dominant theme at their various professional meetings – and remains so until the US penal system is normalized. And the huge research foundations – the Rockefeller Foundation, the Ford Foundation – where are they when they do not see the challenge of bringing the inner workings of their state in order? How is it that the various professional groups within the universities and within the prisons do not convert to activist groups to change the US system into normality?

I would not necessarily be so open in my criticism when visiting totalitarian states. Clear talk, particularly clear public talk, might lead to immediate loss of contact. And it might bring our opposite numbers in such countries into serious trouble, sometimes danger. In prison research or in research on various forms of unacceptable behaviour, we all know well that we have an obligation to protect our sources. But so is also the case when our sources are persons who work in states where they might be severely punished. The Russian poet Anna Achmatova got into severe trouble being visited and embraced by British admirers. Visiting such states demands more self-censorship than visiting the US. I believe this difference is to the pride of the US.

At the same time this means that we are both free and obliged to be outspoken when we meet our US colleagues. We are obliged to expose our concern.

*   *   *

Criminologists have an extraordinary potential for being dangerous people. No wonder that Foucault was sceptical. Some among us work close to power and also close to the intentional delivery of pain. We might easily become technicians in pain delivery of a magnitude and scale in sharp contrast to central values. On the other hand, closeness to power might be an asset. It might give an opportunity to inform the state of the deplorable position of its penal system, when that system is seen in relation to values and civility.

There are probably more criminologists and other experts in this field in the US alone than in all other countries together. Several work precariously close to a deplorable system. Some work within it. They are implicated by proximity and therefore natural targets for blame from abroad.

At the same time, I know, of course I know, that large numbers of US colleagues, perhaps the majority, share many of these views on the US penal system. They know that prisons are universities of crime, and that it is better to invest in ordinary universities. They know that it weakens life in the inner cities to place so many of their inhabitants in the inner life of prisons. They know, and many speak out[5] but feel completely powerless. Realistically so. Maybe the waves from butterfly wings over Italy can create cyclones in the Sahara, but it is difficult to imagine that lectures on crime at Berkeley can change behaviour in Washington – if these lectures are not tuned into the interests of the rulers.

Home from the Soviet Union in the olden days, or from Russia or other countries in Eastern Europe now, I often have had the feeling of having been listened to. I think the visits might have been of some use, not much, but maybe one small impulse among several, for those working close to the penal system. Maybe this is because I am a strange bird in those settings; not so many say what I am saying. Maybe it relates to their position in what the Eastern Europeans call the 'intelligentsia', a group of considerable influence. Or it might these days, as I have mentioned earlier, be related to a genuine wish to come closer to Western European standards. But this is not the urge in the US. They *are* the standards. It is not difficult to understand that many US colleagues give in, shy away from blaming their system for its horrors.

*   *   *

One other mitigating factor related to the responsibility of US colleagues: Europe might soon follow. There are more criminologists in the US, but Europe is on the same track, adapting to modern times both in the development inside the system of punishment, and when it comes to possibilities for academic criticism of this development. I can use conditions in my own country as an illustration.

8.6 The lost heritage of universities

We know the consequences of the social changes taking place. But we do not speak out, not often, not strongly. It sounds so impractical what we can say, so much against the spirit of our time. We censor ourselves so as not to feel completely out of tune. Basically, what we can say, is that if we want to curb penal growth, we have to retard the growth of the one-dimensional society. We must put on the brakes for the dominant position of the economic institution. Development is a fake. There are probably no alternatives, except a retreat to social forms where we, to a large extent, relate to each other as persons, not only as role incumbents. Also in such an existence we will kill each other. Paradise is one floor up. But we will become less like de-linked isolates than when living under conditions where the penal apparatus becomes the only and obvious answer.

In addition to this general advice, we would have to come forward with all the trivial truths described in Chapter 5 – conductors in the subways, no more supermarkets, building up local neighbourhoods, and particularly, mediation instead of delivery of pain.

These are not the easiest of messages to convey, not even inside the universities.

* * *

Those of us in the relatively safe havens of the universities have criminology students. These students will enter the labour market. They want to enter with knowledge they think will be asked for. More theoretical knowledge about crime and crime control is not of obvious importance for the jobs our students will apply for and it will not necessarily be received with enthusiasm by those who are to recruit them. Chances are great that this influences what we, the teachers, write and say. In particular, it might influence what we advise the students to read.

In the 1950s and 1960s, periods with few teachers and only a daring little group of students, and with limited social and political attention to our whereabouts, thinking on radical alternatives became a natural part of scientific existence. But then, slowly, came the increase in the number of students, the need for jobs for these students and the felt need for a curriculum seen as useful in their future jobs. This might be in the ministries, in the municipal administrations, and now, more and more, in the police, the probation services or the prisons.

Criminology is at present trapped in its own success. Jobs for researchers are dependent on jobs for students, which depend on the type of training that makes them useful for jobs in the very institutions we are professionally equipped to raise questions about. Stan Cohen (1988) was right in much of his fierce criticism in his book *Against Criminology*. All have not gone wrong, yet. Universities are, luckily, heavy organizations to change. But the situation is particularly difficult these days.

Universities are just now under extraordinarily strong pressure to prove that they are useful and deserve their money. But good universities should not first and foremost be useful in an immediate practical way. Universities should function as bases for scouts in unknown land and warn when there are dangers ahead. Developments in criminology, but also to a large extent in social sciences in general, are unpleasant examples of dangers when universities are forced to, or voluntarily, take on, the task of serving their states, as these states are and as these states see themselves at any particular moment in time.

Central here is that universities also are trapped in the mono-institutional situation described in Chapter 2. Universities also have to a considerable extent been forced to take on elements similar to those we find in other organizations operating in the markets. Increasingly, universities are organized as if they were factories or shops. They advertise to get students, they promise to provide an education that will prove useful to these students, and the various units are to some extent paid according to the number of students who apply, and later pass examinations.

To attract the best students, it is important to acquire research money. There is a great amount of money available inside the control industry. Police Departments are in need of help, so are prisons and control units outside of prisons. Providers of money for research, access to information and jobs for the students – to a large extent it comes from the very same institution we are supposed to be free to examine and free to criticize.

We also know that if we do not answer the questions raised by the general political system, some other types of researchers will eagerly take our place. As Feeley (2003) points out, the great change in perspective from welfare-criminology to control-criminology in the US was first and foremost a result of the ideas and attitudes of the new researchers drawn from the military experts and their like:

> Those who picked up Wilson's ideas and ran with them were the whiz kids from the Institute of Defense Analysis and RAND. They grafted crime-specific planning and such ideas as defensible space, situational crime prevention and crime-specific planning onto system analysis and cost-benefit analysis, and established the new criminology. Probably the single greatest influence at the national level was the promotion of this new way of thinking. These are the intellectual roots of the new criminology and the new culture of control.
>
> (p. 121)

In a society preoccupied with what is seen as 'the crime problem', this whole situation is particularly difficult. Social science in general, and studies of deviance and social control in particular, are in grave danger. It is as if those supposed to protect our ancient institution do not see what is about to happen when market forces have invaded our universities; what they lose, what researchers lose, and what society loses. By the enormous strength of the market thinking, that old-fashioned institution for the protection of free thought is about to lose its critical potential. The emphasis on our independence and academic freedom is not only an ornament exposed on inauguration day. Independence is a condition for the preservation of our critical ability.

8.7 The need for distance

Come out of the ivory tower, say so many. But we are out. Let us come in again, would be my answer. At a minimum, let us also have the ivory tower. We cannot only be in. Distance is a necessity to see the whole perspective.

We must also be out. But then we are soon in trouble. Let me reveal some experience from working with these problems in a small country such as mine.

I believe that our Norwegian penal system is much too large. We could do with a much smaller prison population. We could also have prisons with emphasis on more civil forms of interaction. We could use mediation and restoration to find civil solutions to a great number of conflicts now handled by the penal system. We have allowed our penal system to grow when a great number of the problems could have been prevented by increased emphasis on social welfare. This is my basic position, one shared by many of my colleagues.

But at the same time, I am of course in continuous contact with those operating the penal law system, as I am with those being operated on there. I lecture for prisoners as well as for guards, and for police and judges. They invite us in as we invite them. We have now and then joint seminars with prisoners and guards or with prisoners alone. I feel pretty sure that there would not be any prison in Norway today, where I would not be welcomed if I asked to be let in. It has not always been like that. Once, in the early 1970s, Professor Vilhelm Aubert and I were refused a meeting with prisoners in a particular prison. It became a scandal, the refusal came before Parliament, but the decision was not changed. It would not have happened today.

Then, as we all know, social contact works both ways. We teach, but are also taught. We influence, and we become influenced. And personal attachments are created. I *like* a great number of those persons I meet within these systems, from prisoners to prison directors. I find no monsters among prisoners, nor do I find them among those running the systems. On the contrary, I meet many dedicated persons doing their utmost to combine the tasks of functioning as guards and at the same time making life bearable for those they guard. The employees in the crime control system read our books. They get some of our perspective. But we also get theirs. They might have concrete problems, and we attempt to answer them. They might have more general questions, suited for research, and we take part in a dialogue on possible research designs. We come close to each other. They are the persons who deliver the pain. And we help to make it possible.

Is this co-operation right?

I will say, it cannot be otherwise. The penal system is our major field of study. We have to come close, to see. But being so close, we might be blinded.

*   *   *

When criminology was young in Norway, a leading forensic psychiatrist told me how much he regretted that the Institute of Criminology was situated at the University of Oslo in the centre of town. We ought to have had our premises in a nearby prison. Here were the prisoners, our objects for study. Those we were to explain.

To me, this episode made a great impression. It told me a lesson of the danger inherent in claims that we ought to be useful according to premises established by specialists within the penal system. I ended up writing a little article on the relationship between prisons and various sorts of specialists who might be useful for prisoners or prison administrators (Christie 1970). I compared two ideal-typical models for the relationship between specialists and prisons: the self-sufficiency model and the importation model. Take the doctors; they can be an integrated part of the prison services, or a part of the general health services of the municipality. So also with teachers; they can be attached to the general school system of the municipality, with the school director as the boss, or they can be a part of the prison system, with prison directors in command. The importation model is the one where all these specialists belong to the external world, but are invited in, imported, into the prisons. It is a system where the specialists retain their identification with the outside world, keep the standards out there as standards for work, and also are free to resist demands from the prison staff if these demands are not in accordance with their professional standards.

This actually became the dominant model in Norway. But now the pendulum is swinging back. The educational level is steadily increasing in all areas of the nation, and schools for prison officers fall in line. The prison school has recently asked for college status. The education here lasts three years after high school. The prison guards feel more qualified these days and take on tasks close to therapeutic ones after attending some extra courses. Various experts teach at the school. A unit for research is attached. A similar development is taking place within the police. Their school has already attained college status, with a research unit attached. They get their 'own' professors in 2003. Little by little, the penal law system again becomes self-sufficient.

Fine. Increased quality among those working in the penal system. But at the very same time, it is a dangerous development. Those working there – from guards in prisons to teachers at these schools – will to a larger extent be captured in the system. They will not be completely free (or motivated) to shout about failures, and particularly not to resist growth of the system – their home base.

The particular danger in the situation is that it all happens at the very same time when the universities are converting to market institutions.

When we need them most, the protective shields are taken away. From a theoretical point of view, the whole development is a fascinating confirmation of the power of the one-dimensional society. From the perspective among those of us with a strong wish for preserving room for free criticism, it is a most alarming development.

* * *

All this is true. But it is not the whole truth. There are cracks in the wall. The hegemony is not quite total. Maybe markets cannot take us all the way. Maybe creation is more important than money. Maybe new generations of university people will gather to rebuild parts of the ivory tower. There will always be some protesters around.

8.8 Individual resistance

The villages for extraordinary people described in Chapter 2 can in a way be seen as small kernels of resistance. Other exampmles are the Mennonites and the Amish people in Canada and the USA, the Jewish settlements in the old Eastern Europe, or tribes stuck away in deep jungles. They survive the dominant monolithic culture of our time by hiding, or by the creation of counter-cultures.

This shows the importance of community. But this insight might easily create pessimism. It can lead us to forget the importance of individual actions. Therefore, what now follows are some small stories with the only purpose of re-creating trust in the single individual.

Far back in time, I met a man who taught me a lesson about freedom. He had received a prison sentence that he found deeply unjust, and went on hunger strike. He was transported to an isolation cell at the very bottom of the prison. His clothes were removed to prevent suicide. Tempting meals were brought to him, but in vain. He was then fed by force, but got rid of the food by eating his excrement and vomiting. This was before doctors had developed their more sophisticated methods for forced feeding. The prison director came down to him. The director cried, and begged him to eat. The man's comments to me were these: 'I have never felt so free. Nothing more could be taken away from me.'

Mauricio Rosencoff is an acquaintance. He is from Uruguay. In eleven years he – and ten other men – were kept in complete isolation by the military junta of the country. International attention prevented their killing, but not the torture and the totality of their isolation. For periods, they got almost no water. To survive, they had to drink their own urine. To survive as human beings, nearly all of them engaged in some sort of cultural activity. Mauricio Rosencoff wrote poetry in his head. At one stage, he got hold of a pencil and was able to smuggle out his poems on small bits of paper. When he was released, he found out he had become a famous poet in Uruguay. 'They treated us as dogs,' said Mauricio. 'But we did not bark back.' Later, we had a seminar in Oslo on torture. Mauricio took part. So did also a man who had acted as a torturer in Uruguay. After the seminar, they went out, the two of them, for a meal together.

Janina Bauman is the third carrier of stubborn humanity to be mentioned here. She survived the German invasion of Poland. She survived the Warsaw ghetto, escaped, and survived anew in hiding outside the ghetto. And she also survived living with memories. Forty years after it all, she wrote her beautiful, terrible book *Winter in the Morning* (1986), the book that inspired her husband, Zygmunt Bauman, to write his book on *Modernity and the Holocaust* (1989). And Janina developed the theme even further in the autumn of 1992 at our Institute in Oslo when she gave a seminar with the title: 'To survive with dignity'. She is an example, herself.[6]

Not even prisons, which we rightly enough call total institutions, not even they are completely total. The naked prisoner survived by keeping control over his own body. Mauricio Rosencoff survived by creating poems. Janina Bauman survived – particularly the years after the Holocaust – by giving words to what had happened.

So, this is my contribution to hope in this work. Totalitarian powers are not in total command, even under the most extreme of conditions. Not inside the prisons, not inside the ghetto, not inside the totalitarian state. Some humans make the choice to live, and eventually to die, with dignity.

Notes

Roots

1 Christie (1952/1974).
2 Christie (1960).
3 Christie and Bruun (1985/2003).
4 Christie (1993/2000).
5 A note on language. I write here in English but fight to preserve my native Norwegian melody. Anne Turner, my kind and patient guide in English, has had to accept expressions closer to my rhythms than to what is usually acceptable to traditional guardians of the English language. I am grateful for her tolerance. What might sound 'foreign' in what here follows, are not her mistakes, only my attempts to preserve my linguistic form. I continue (see Christie 1981) to act as if England has lost her property right to her language.

1 Crime does not exist

1 Thanks to Cecilie Høigård for stubborn resistance to some earlier suggestions.
2 Prison figures have existed back to 1814.
3 *Dagens Nyheter*, 13 and 14 March 1997.
4 This was a burning topic, maybe first and foremost among German/Austrian sociologists and criminologists in the 1980s and 1990s. I profited much from discussions with Henner Hess, Sebastian Scheerer and Heinz Steinert, all in Frankfurt. Louk Hulsman from Rotterdam was an important inspirator to much of it. An interesting recent contribution from the Max Plank Institute in Freiburg is the book *Images of Crime*, edited by Hans-Jörg Albrecht, Afroditi Koukoutsaki and Telemach Serassis (2001). Of particular relevance here is the article by Serassis on 'The Lost Honour of Criminology: A Documentary of the Vicissitudes of a Discipline'.
5 I construct the case, but not out of the blue. The Swedish anthropologist Åke Daun (1974) has provided much material for the construction. So has also a life lived in these countries.

2 Monocultures

1 As a boy in school I learned that a relative was a well-known man when our constitution came into being in 1814. He died just before my great-aunts were born. I ran to the aunts and asked them to tell me about this great man. They completely refused. He was a non-person. He had lived with a woman he was not married to. Even worse, he had children with her. It did not help that he made them legitimate through a legal act available at that time.

3 The use-value of crime

1 Until the Winter War against the USSR in 1939, males of the labour class in Finland were not given military training. They were not to be trusted.
2 Much due to the writings of Inkeri Anttila and Patrik Törnudd (1973), and Törnudd (1996).
3 The Norwegian situation is not much better, see Frantzen (2001). For a general description of the drug policy in the Nordic countries, see Christie and Bruun (2003). The book is available in the major Nordic languages, and in German.
4 For a general description of the UN drug commission, a description that is still valid, see Bruun, Rexed and Pan (1975).
5 Finland has 5 million inhabitants.
6 Annually over 300,000 Russian automobiles cross the border and hit the Finnish roads (Bäckman 1998b, p. 2).

4 Incarceration as an answer

1 http:/www.kcl.ac.uk/depsta/rel/icps/worldbrief/.
2 Source: Ludmilla Alpern, Moscow Centre for Prison Reform.
3 Kaataja Franko Aas has written a fascinating doctoral thesis on the relationship between technology and sentencing theory and practice (2003).
4 Federal Judicial Centre at http://www.fjc.gov/pubs.html.
5 To me, one person epitomizes the resistance against all this. It is Al Bronstein, legal adviser to black people during their actions in Alabama in the dangerous 1960s. And then, until the present, a central activist against the prison development in the north. Today, he is still an important adviser for Prison Reform International in London.
6 Anton Chekhov (1967) gives a unique description of life among the deported to the island Sakhalin, close to Japan, which was colonized in this way in the 1890s. Chekhov was not there as a prisoner, but as a doctor with social consciousness for his country-fellows. I am most grateful to Ludmilla Alpern who made me aware of this unique penological report.
7 I got the diagram and additional figures from Monika Platek and Pawel Moczydlowski during a week of lectures and seminars in Warsaw, and was also assisted by Klaus Witold and Dagmara Wozniakowska.
8 *Guardian*, 16 June 2003.
9 *The Observer*, 30 March 2003.

6 No punishment

1 Cf. Fangen (2001) and Bjørgo (1997).
2 In February 2003 one of them was sentenced to 17 years of imprisonment, the other 18 years.
3 The term *abolitionism* is inherited from the struggle against slavery, especially in the USA. Within this movement, the conflict was between those who wanted to abolish slavery altogether, and those who, by various means, wished to limit slavery. And, as in the struggle against slavery, a more moderate group also exists within the abolitionist movement. They are the minimalists. It is a bad name from the history of slavery, but a good one confronted with the complexities of finding answers to severely unwanted acts.

7 Answers to atrocities

1 'Mind' – a term which significantly enough means just memory, or in old Norse *minne*.
2 Milosevic might be a bad man, and also be found guilty in a court in Belgrade. I have no opinion on this question. But while I am writing this, it can be clearly observed how Milosevic uses the way he was brought to The Hague as a part in his defence.
3 Penal Reform International, Annual Report 2000, p. 7.
4 For a most clarifying discussion of the relationship between reconciliation and restorative justice, see Parmentier (2001).
5 Thanks to Ragnhild Hennum for her arguments on this point.

8 When is enough, enough?

1 It is an interesting aspect of life that states that might be criticized on criteria (3) and (4) – on volume, and containing a biased prison population – are often the leaders in criticizing states that are deviant on criteria (1) and (2) – on types of crime and forms of decision making.
2 According to Slagstad (1999, p. 456). My translation.
3 John Braithwaite has had an exceptional importance for the development of ideas as well as practice in the field of mediation and restorative justice. His last book, *Restorative Justice and Responsive Regulation* (Braithwaite 2002) is at this stage the most complete account of his work. A particular pleasure in reading Braithwaite is the harmony between content and form. He writes about conciliation. And he uses, even in polemics, an exceptionally peaceful form.
4 Penal Reform International have their major base in London, but also an office in Moscow.
5 I am tempted to mention several persons and organizations by name, but refrain from doing so. It would be so many deserving a place on such a list of honour, and I do not know them all. Therefore, no one mentioned, no one forgotten.
6 Through a comparative analysis of the two major ghettos in Poland during World War II – the one in Warsaw and the other in Lodz – she was also

able to point to those social-structural factors which increase the possibilities for the protection of human dignity under extreme conditions. Her major theme in this analysis was that a social system which puts utility above values is in grave danger of destroying both life and dignity.

References

Aas, Katja Franko (2003) *From Faust to Macintosh: Sentencing in the Age of Information*. Institute of Criminology and Sociology of Law, University of Oslo.

Åkerström, Malin (2000) 'Det gicks Bärsärkargång' – nedtoning av våld på sjukhem. Pp. 297–319 in Ingrid Sahlin and Malin Åkerström (eds) *Det lokala våldet. Om rädsla, rasism och social kontroll*. Liber, Stockholm.

Åkerström, Malin (2002) Slaps, Punches, Pinches – But not Violence: Boundary-work in Nursing Homes for the Elderly. *Symbolic Interaction*, Vol. 25, No. 4, pp. 515–36.

Albrecht, Hans-Jörg, Afroditi Koukoutsaki and Telemach Serassis (2001) *Images of Crime*, Kriminologische Forschungsberichte aus dem Max-Planck-Institut für Ausländisches und Internationales Strafrecht, Band 97. Freiburg.

Anttila, Inkeri and Patrik Törnudd (1973) *Kriminologi i kriminalpolitisk perspektiv*. Norstedt, Stockholm.

Aromaa, Kauko and Andri Ahven (1995) *Victims of Crime in a Time of Change: Estonia 1993 and 1995*. National Research Institute of Legal Policy, Research Communications, Helsinki.

Aromaa, Kauko and Martti Lehti (1995) *The Security of Finnish Companies in St. Petersburg*. National Research Institute of Legal Policy, Helsinki.

Bäckman, Johan (1998a) *The Inflation of Crime in Russia: The Social Danger of the Emerging Markets*. National Research Institute of Legal Policy, Helsinki.

Bäckman, Johan (1998b) *The Inflation of Crime in Russia*. Presentation in a seminar organized by Scandinavian Research Council for Criminology. Espo, Finland.

Baldursson, Erlendur (2000) Prisoners, Prisons and Punishment in Small Societies. *Journal of Scandinavian Studies in Criminology and Crime Prevention*, Vol. 1, pp. 6–15.

Bauman, Janina (1986) *Winter in the Morning*. Virago, London; Free Press, New York.

Bauman, Zygmunt (1989) *Modernity and the Holocaust*. Polity Press, Cambridge.

Bauman, Zygmunt (1998) *Globalization: The Human Consequences*. Polity Press, Cambridge.

Bauman, Zygmunt (2000) Social Issues of Law and Order. *British Journal of Criminology*, Vol. 40, pp. 205–221.

Bennet, Jamie (2003) Winston Churchill. Prison Reformer? *Prison Service Journal*, No. 145, pp. 3–7.

Bjørgo, Tore (1997) *Racist and Right-Wing Violence in Scandinavia: Patterns, Perpetrators, and Responses.* Aschehoug, Oslo.

Bottoms, Anthony E. and Paul Wiles (1992) Explanations of Crime and Place. Pp. 11–35 *Crime, Policing and Place: Essays in Environmental Criminology.* Routledge, London.

Braithwaite, John (2002) *Restorative Justice and Responsive Regulation.* Oxford University Press, Oxford.

Bruun, Kettil, Ingemar Rexed and Lynn Pan (1975) *Gentlemen's Club: International Control of Drugs and Alcohol.* The University of Chicago Press, Chicago.

Chekhov, Anton (1967) *The Island: A Journey to Sakhalin.* Introduction by Irena Ratushinskaya. Washington Square Press. (In 1987 Century, an imprint of Century Hutchinson Ltd, London.)

Christianson, Scott (1998) *With Liberty for Some: 500 Years of Imprisonment in America.* Northeastern University Press, USA.

Christie, Nils (1952/1974) *Fangevoktere i konsentrasjonsleir.* Pax, Oslo.

Christie, Nils (1960) *Tvangsarbeid og alkoholbruk,* Universitetsforlaget, Oslo.

Christie, Nils (1970) Modeller for fengselsorganisasjonen. In Rita Østensen (ed.) *I stedet for fengsel.* Pax, Oslo.

Christie (1973) A Living Society is a Quarrelling Society. In *Law and Social Change.* Annual Lecture Series 1971/1972. Osgoode Hall Law School, York University.

Christie, Nils (1981) *Limits to Pain.* Martin Robertson, Oxford.

Christie, Nils and Kettil Bruun (1985/2003) *Den gode fiende.* Third revised edn. Universitetsforlaget, Oslo. German edition: *Der nützliche Feind,* AJZ (1991).

Christie, Nils (1987) *Beyond Loneliness and Institutions: Communes for Extraordinary People.* Scandinavian University Press, Oslo.

Christie, Nils (1993/2000) *Crime Control as Industry: Towards Gulags, Western Style.* Third edn. Routledge, London.

Cohen, Albert K. (1955) *Delinquent Boys: The Culture of the Gang.* The Free Press, New York.

Cohen, Stan (1988) *Against Criminology.* Transaction Books, New Brunswick.

Cooley, Charles Horton (1902) *Human Nature and the Social Order.* Charles Scribner, New York.

Dahrendorf, Ralf (1985) *Law and Order.* The Hamlyn Lectures, 37. Steven, London.

Daun, Åke (1974) *Förortsliv: en etnologisk studie av kulturell förändring.* Prisma, Stockholm.

Dearden, Lorraine, Alissa Goodman and Phillippa Saunders (2003) Income and Living Standards. Pp. 148–93 in Elsa Ferri, John Bynner and Michael Wadsworth (eds) *Changing Britain, Changing Lives: Three Generations at the Turn of the Century.* Institute of Education, London.

Dobroszycki, Lucjan (1984) The Chronicle of the Lodz Ghetto 1941–1944. Yale University Press, New Haven, London.

Donziger, Steven R. (1996) The Real War on Crime: The Report of the National Criminal Justice Commission. Harper Perennial, New York.

Ellingsen, Dag (1993) Krigsprofitørene og rettsoppgjøret. Gyldendal, Oslo.

Enzenberger, Hans Magnus (1985) Ach Europa! Suhrkamp Verlag, Frankfurt am Main. In Norwegian: Akk Europa! Inntrykk fra syv land med en epilog fra år 2006. Universitetsforlaget, Oslo (1987).

Enzenberger, Hans Magnus (1989) Tilbaketogets helte. Moderne Tider, 29 December 1989, Copenhagen.

Estrada, Felipe (1999) Ungdomsbrottslighet som samhällsproblem. Kriminologiska institutionen, Stockholms universitetet. Avhandlingsserie No. 3.

Estrada, Felipe (2001) Juvenile Violence as a Social Problem. British Journal of Criminology, Vol. 41, pp. 639–55.

Fangen, Katrine (2001) Pride and Power: A Sociological Study of the Norwegian Radical Nationalist Underground Movement. Institutt for sosiologi og samfunnsgeografi, Universitetet i Oslo.

Feeley, Malcolm (2003) Crime, Social Order and the Rise of Neo-Conservative Politics. Theoretical Criminology, Vol. 7, pp. 111–130.

Foucault, Michel (1977) Discipline and Punish: The Birth of the Prison. Vintage, New York.

Frantzen, Evy (2001) Metadonmakt: Møtet mellom narkotikabrukere og norsk metadonpolitikk. Universitetsforlaget, Oslo.

Garland, David (2001) The Culture of Control: Crime and Social Order in Contemporary Society. Oxford University Press, Oxford.

Gezelius, Stig Strandli (2002) Legitimacy, Compliance, Survival: Natural Resource Harvesters and the State. Rapport 1: 2002 Institutt for sosiologi og samfunnsgeografi, Universitetet i Oslo.

Giertsen, Hedda (2003) Straff er ikke noe rensemiddel. To be printed in To the celebration of Thomas Mathiesen. Pax, Oslo.

Gilinsky, Yakov (1997) Organized Crime in Russia: Theory and Practice. Security Journal, Vol. 9, pp. 165–9.

Haddad, Angela (2003) Critical Reflexivity, Contradictions and Modern Cuban Consciousness. Acta Sociologica, Vol. 46, pp. 51–68.

Hagtvet, Bernt (1981) Totalitarianisme. PaxLeksikon, Vol. 6, pp. 285–6. Pax, Oslo.

Hawkins, Gordon (1969) God and the Mafia. The Public Interest, Vol. 14, pp. 24–51.

Hobsbawm, E.J. (1994) Age of Extremes: The Short Twentieth Century 1914–1991. Michael Joseph, London.

Homans, George Caspar (1951) The Human Group. Routledge & Kegan Paul, London.

Høigård, Cecilie (2002) Gategallerier. Pax, Oslo.

Illich, Ivan (1992) Needs. In Wolfgang Sachs (ed.) The Development Dictionary: A Guide to Knowledge as Power. Zed Books, London.

Kalinin, Yuri Ivanovich (2002) *The Russian Penal System: Past, Present and Future*. Kings College London, International Centre for Prison Studies.

King, Roy D. (1999) The Rise and Rise of Supermax: An American Solution in Search of a Problem? *Punishment and Society*, Vol. 1, No. 2, pp. 163–86.

Klein, Ernest (1971) *Comprehensive Etymological Dictionary of the English Language*. Elsevier, Amsterdam.

Kovalev, Sergei (2000) Putin's War. *The New York Review of Books*, 10 February, Vol. XLVII, No. 2, pp. 4–8.

Linz, Juan (1975) USA Totalitarian and Authoritarian Regimes. In Fred I. Greenstein and Nelson W. Polsby (eds) *Handbook of Political Science*, Vol. 3. Addison-Wesley, Reading, Mass.

Los, Maria (2002) Post-Communist Fear of Crime and the Commercialization of Security. *Theoretical Criminology*, Vol. 6, No. 2, pp. 165–88.

Los, Maria and Adrzej Zybertowizh (2000) *Privatizing the Police-State: The Case of Poland*. Macmillan, Basingstoke.

Mathiesen, Thomas (1985) *The Defences of the Weak. A Sociological Study of a Norwegian Correctional Institution*. Tavistock, London.

Mathiesen, Thomas (1997) The Viewer Society; Foucault's 'Panopticon' Revisited. *Theoretical Criminology*, Vol. 1, No. 2, pp. 215–34.

Mauer, Marc (1999) *Race to Incarcerate*. New Press, New York.

Mauer, Marc and Meda Chesney-Lind (2002) *Invisible Punishment: The Collateral Consequences of Mass Imprisonment*. New Press, New York.

Miszal, Barbara A. (2001). Legal Attempts to Construct Collective Memory. *Polish Sociological Review*, 1 (133).

Moscow Helsinki Group (2003) *Situation of Prisoners in Contemporary Russia*. Moscow Helsinki Group in co-operation with the International Helsinki Federation for Human Rights, the Netherlands Helsinki Committee and the Polish Helsinki Foundation for Human Rights. Moscow.

Nader, Laura (2002) *The Life of the Law: Anthropological Projects*. University of California Press, Berkeley, Los Angeles, London.

Neuberger, Joan (1993) *Hooliganism: Crime, Culture and Power in St. Petersburg, 1900– 1914*. University of California Press, Berkeley.

Olsen, Kåre (1998) *Krigens barn: de norske krigsbarna og deres mødre*. Aschehoug, Oslo.

Østerberg, Dag (1991) Universitetet og vitenskap i dagens samfunn. In Egil A. Wyller (ed.) *Universitetets idé gjennom tidene og i dag: en samling Oslo-foredrag*. Universitetsforlaget, Oslo.

Panuk, Orham (2001) The Anger of the Damned. *New York Review of Books*, 15 Nov., pp. 12–15.

Parmentier, Stephan (2001) The South African Truth and Reconciliation Commission: Towards Restorative Justice in the Field of Human Rights. In E. Fattah and S. Parmentier (Eds) *Victim Policies and Criminal Justice on the Road to Restorative Justice: Essays in Honour of Tony Peters*. Leuven, Belgium.

Piacentini, Laura Francesca (2002) *Work to Live: The Function of Prison Labour in the Russian Prison System*. Doctoral dissertation, Bangor University, Wales.

Putnam, Robert D. (2000) Bowling Alone: The Collapse and Revival of American Community. Simon & Schuster, New York.

Rawlinson, Patricia (1998) Mafia, Media and Myth. The Howard Journal, Vol. 37, No. 4, pp. 346–58.

Sahlin, Ingrid (2003) Review of: Lise-Lotte Rytterbro, Medling – möten med Möjligheter: En analys av en nygammal reaktion på brott. Nordisk Tidsskrift for Kriminalvidenskab, Vol. 90, No. 2, pp. 135–41.

Sharpe, Andrew (2000) A Comparison of Canadian and US Labour Market Performance in the 1990s. In Maureen Appel Molot and Fen Osler Hampson (eds) Vanishing Borders. Canada Among Nations 2000. Oxford University Press, Oxford.

Schmidt-Häuer (2000) In Namen der Völker. Die Zeit/Morgenbladet, 5–11 July.

Shelley, Louise (1980) The Geography of Soviet Criminality. American Sociological Review, Vol. 45, pp. 111–22.

Shelley, Louise (1994) Post-Soviet Organized Crime: Implications for Economic, Social and Political Development. Demokratizatsiya, Vol. II, No. 3, pp. 341–58, US. Excerpts in Trends in Organized Crime, Vol. 1, 1995, pp. 7–20.

Simon, Jonathan (2004) Governing Through Crime. (Not yet published)

Simmel, George (1990) The Philosophy of Money. Routledge, London.

Skardhamar, Torbjørn (1998) Grafitti – estetikk og kulturell motstand. Institutt for kriminologi, Universitetet i Oslo. Stensilserien No. 90.

Slagstad, Rune (1999) De nasjonale strateger. Pax, Oslo.

Steinert, Heinz (1986) Beyond Crime and Punishment. Contemporary Crises, Vol. 10, pp. 21–38. See also his preface (1986) entitled Abolitionismus: Die harte Wirklichkeit und der Möglichkeitssinn to Nils Christie, Grenzen des Leids, AJZ Verlag, Bielefeld, pp. 1–13.

Stern, Vivian, ed. (1999) Sentenced to Die? The Problem of TB in Prisons in Eastern Europe and Central Asia. International Centre for Prison Studies, King's College, London.

Suominen, Tapani (1996) 'Verre enn Quislings hird': metaforiska kamper i den offentliga debatten kring 1960- och 1970-talens student- och ungdomsradikalism i Norge, Finland och Västtytskland. Doctoral Dissertation, Institute of Criminology and Sociology of Law, Oslo.

Tham, Henrik (1995) Drug Control as a National Project: The Case of Sweden. Journal of Drug Issues, Vol. 25, No. 1, pp 113–28.

Tham, Henrik (2001) Law and Order as a Leftist Project? The Case of Sweden. Punishment and Society, Vol. 3, No. 3, pp. 409–26.

Tham, Henrik (2003) Forskare om narkotikapolitiken. Stockholm.

Törnudd, Patrik (1996) Fifteen Years of Decreasing Prisoners Rates in Finland. The National Research Institute of Legal Policy, Helsinki.

Walmsley, Roy (2003) World Prison Population List. Findings, 188, Home Office, London.

Ylikangas, Heikki (1995) Vägen til Tammerfors: striden mellan röda och vita i finska innbördeskriget 1918. Söderström, Helsinki.

Index